Cor

MW01383759

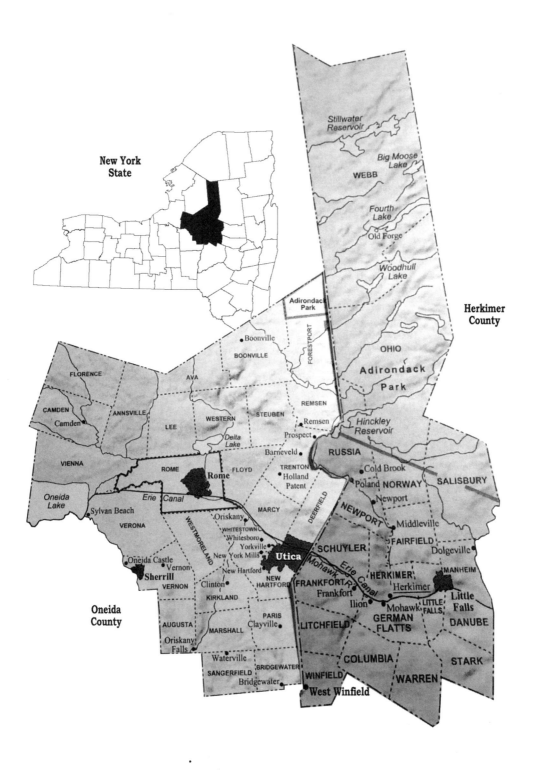

Women Belong in History Books

Herkimer and Oneida Counties
1700-1950

Edited by Jane Sullivan Spellman - 2015

Jane Sullivan Spellman
10/25/2015

ISBN: 978-1-4951-6778-2

Library of Congress number is pending

Printed in the US by Vicks
Book Layout by Robert Jenkins

Photos on Front Cover:

Top (left to right):
Libby Sherman Kowalsky
Catherine Milet Buckley
Silvia Saunders

Middle (left to right):
Josephine Young Case
Zaida Zoller
Saint Marianne Cope

Bottom (left to right):
Ellen Clapsaddle
Corinne Roosevelt Robinson
Helen Munson Williams

Photos on Back Cover:

Top (left to right):
Jessie Moon Holton
Grace Van Wagenen Carpenter
Welthy Honsinger Fisher

Middle (left to right):
Mary Cornelius Winder
Grace Cogswell Root
Loretta O. Douglas

Third (left to right):
Charlotte Buell Coman
Lucy Carlile Watson
Harriet A. Ackroyd

Bottom (left to right):
Helene Chadwick
Rose Cleveland

To my mother,

Ruth Reedy Sullivan

1903-1982

and her mother,

Anastasia Fogarty Reedy

1871-1942

Who knew

women could do anything.

INTRODUCTION

The beginning of this book to record remarkable women in Herkimer and Oneida Counties began in 1987 when the Herkimer County Historical Society decided a new county history was needed. The last one was published in 1893, and as the County approached the 200th anniversary of its beginning in 1791, a new publication seemed appropriate.

Fortunately Josephine Case and her husband, Bob Mason, had recently retired to Herkimer County and Josephine agreed to be the editor. Josephine, a graduate of Bryn Mawr and Oxford University, was, among other positions, the assistant editor for the Metropolitan Museum of Art Bulletin. Bob, a Lafayette College graduate, was writer and editor of the Newark, New Jersey Evening News and Director of Employee Communications for the American Telephone and Telegraph Company in New York City. Under their leadership, *Herkimer County at 200* was published in 1992. It was not planned that way, but the number of women involved in the new history was impressive: the editor, photography editor, timeline editor and authors of five of the six chapters were women, as well as the publisher. It is also noted the HCHS President and Chairman of the Publications Committee at the time were women. It is great to quote the review that this book got from NEW YORK HISTORY, the quarterly publication of the New York State Historical Association, Cooperstown, NY, which calls *Herkimer County at 200* "the best of the best".

As the 19th century histories were reviewed, it was apparent all had been written by men who wrote of the things important to them. Men came, settled and their sons married and communities grew. Rarely are women mentioned by name. This new history would include women.

However, the difficulty of doing research was enormous. The federal census only recorded the head of the household from the first one in 1790 to 1850. If church records were available, women's names are recorded, but many ministers moved and took the records with them. When a girl married, she became a part of another family, but she usually kept records of her own family. It took researchers years to look to the women for information on their own family. The best one could do was learn what was happening at the time and what was accomplished, then put the individual woman in the setting. Identifying women's organizations and learning their histories began to help create the background needed to show the individual's contribution.

Research in national, regional and local associations began. A timeline was created and the search for individuals commenced.

I retired in 1995 as Director of the Herkimer County Historical Society with the intention of continuing more research, but several consulting jobs, travel and family involvement made the study a slow one.

In 1998, Lynne Mishalanie began UTICA MONDAY NITE and asked me to give a 14 week course on "200 Years of Great Women" at the Utica Public Library. It seemed sensible to add Oneida County women to the study and the wonderful group of men and women who attended the classes were generous with suggestions and the list began. The list reached 100 women, research done on 55, essays were written on 20 and I was out of energy.

Then in July 2014, Lynne Mishalanie called and asked me to give a program on local women as part of a series she and Dr. Kathleen Bishop were presenting for the Mohawk Valley Institute for Learning in Retirement. Lynne and Kathie volunteered to get this publication back on track. Their wonderful enthusiasm and know-how developed a plan to recruit interested people to finish the research and write the essays using the same format. Judy Gorman joined the team to raise money and get us moving ahead.

The decision to use the years 1700-1950 was arbitrary, but 20th century records are available. Since the book was to have room for a timeline, source material and photos, it would run about 300 pages. It was decided to publish Volume1 and have this book earn enough money to finish the remaining biographical essays in Volume 2.

The joy of seeing this first publication a reality is incredible and hopefully the many people, especially the other writers, who have made this first volume possible, will feel as rewarded as I do for the knowledge this project has provided.

You are reading the results. Do enjoy getting to know these wonderful local women who have been put into the history books.

Jane Sullivan Spellman

April 2015

WRITERS

None of this would have been possible without the over twenty years of research and dedication to this topic by Jane Spellman. The volumes of information she has gathered led the wonderfully talented and dedicated writers of this book to not only write up the information but also to add more research of their own. Each has a different story to tell about their journey related to this book. It has been an honor to work on this project together to make it happen and I remain grateful to all of them and this opportunity to help put some of the women of Herkimer and Oneida Counties into history books.

Kathleen M. Bishop, Ph. D.

Shirley Tucker Burtch	Oriskany
Mary Anne Luebbert Buteux	New Hartford
Anna Tobin D'Ambrosio	New Hartford
Jane Winterbotton Dieffenbacher	Fairfield
Barbara Sabo Dunadee	Ilion
Caryl Darling Hopson	Dolgeville
Virginia Baird Kelly	Utica
Lori Gabriel Knapp	Frankfort
B. Ann Lewis Maher	Newport
Peg Nash Masters	Old Forge
Joyce Fellows Murphy	Middleville
Susan R. Perkins	Dolgeville
Susan Stevens Radell	Whitesboro
Donna Loomis Rubin	Millers Mills
Janice Trimbey Reilly	New Hartford
Marjorie E. Sabo	Peekskill
Jane Sullivan Spellman	Ilion
Susan Guzik Tice	Whitesboro
Roberta Seaton Walsh	Newport
Kandice Watson	Oneida
Richard L. Williams	Clinton

TIMELINE AND TABLE OF CONTENTS

1793	Oneida Academy opened. It will become Hamilton College in 1812. Holland Land Company began to sell land in Barnevelt.
1794	NYS Legislature authorized the building of the Great Genesee Road from Old Fort Schuyler (Utica) west to the Genesee Valley.
1797	Oneida County was formed from Herkimer County. Old Fort Schuyler became village of Utica with fifty houses.
1799	The Cherry Valley Turnpike (Route 20) chartered from Albany to Cazenovia.

1803	Fairfield Academy opened in Fairfield, NY. Herkimer County Medical Society organized. Military Road built from Albany to Sackets Harbor.

1809	One of the earliest cotton mills in NYS began in New York Mills.
1811	A woolen mill, believed to be the first in NYS, built in Oriskany.

1812-1814	War of 1812.
1816	Female Missionary Society of Utica held first meeting. Remington Arms Company started in the Ilion Gorge.
1817-1825	Construction of the Erie Canal began in Rome.

1833	Mothers Magazine, printed in Utica, created a network between Maternal Associations in rural and urban areas throughout the US.
1836-1926	**Anna Perkins,** Educator/Librarian - Ilion.
1836	The Chenango Canal opened from Utica to Binghamton.
1837-1894	**Lomy Redfield Proctor,** Community Leader - Utica.
1838-1918	**Saint Marianne Cope,** Missionary - Utica.................................52
1838-1910	**Martha DeEtte Brown Lincoln,** Author - Columbia.
1838-1918	**Helen Case Waite,** Community Leader - Little Falls.
1838-1915	**Julia Chester Goddard Platt,** Educator - Utica.
1839	The Utica Schenectady Railroad became operational.
1840-1916	**Kate E. Jones,** National Leader - Ilion...54
1840-1931	**Henrietta H. Wright,** Philanthropist - Rome.
1841-1876	**Charlotte Grey Beckwith Crouse,** Community Leader - Utica.
1841-1912	**Blandina Dudley Miller,** Author - Utica.
c1841-1928	**Ellen Elizabeth Lavender,** Evangelist - Utica. 58
1843-1928	**Netti Bowen Smith,** Adventurer - Newport
1843-1898	**Elizabeth Snell Folts,** Community Leader - Herkimer.
1843-1908	**Elizabeth Whipple Gilbert,** Suffragist - Schuyler.
1843	Utica State Hospital opened, the first publicly funded institution for the mentally ill.
1844-1933	**Lodema Washburn Devendorf,** Community Leader - Herkimer.

1937   NYS law passed which allows women to serve on a jury.

1941-1945   World War II.

1942-1993   **Jacqueline McCormack Tolles,** Community
            Leader - New Hartford.

Sources will follow at the end of the essays and the women will
appear alphabetically.

CATHERINE PETRIE HERKIMER

was born in 1700, tradition has it she is the daughter of Johan Jost Petrie and Anna Gertruyd Petrie of Strasburg, Alsace. According to the *Mohawk Valley Petries and Allied Families,* she was baptized on May 5, 1700 at B Church in the southwest part of Germany known as the Palatinate. She was among the 13,000 Germans who left their homeland for religious and economic reasons and went to England. That many refugees in London led Queen Anne to send many refugees as workers to America with hopes of collecting tar to be used for naval vessels. Catherine came to America with her parents as one of the 1710 Palatine Expedition from England to New York Harbor.

Catherine was almost 10 when her family left England with 4,000 others in January of 1710, arriving in New York June 4th. Only 3,400 survived the trip. For a short time the group stayed in New York City whose population was just 6,000. Her family was settled on Livingston Manor along the Hudson River under the supervision of Alyda Schuyler Livingston, whose husband Robert was busy in New York City as a member of the Colonial Legislature. The Schuylers had the contract to house and feed the newcomers and there were many disputes over what the contracts covered. After two years it was decided the native trees were not suitable for the naval project and in September the tar project was cancelled. Support from the English government was cut off. Catherine's family was among those who went over the mountains and claimed land along the Schoharie River, where they survived the winter with the aid of the local Indians. The Palatines cleared the land and planted crops. It was a shock to discover the land they cultivated was claimed by a distant Albany businessmen. Although the Palatines sent representatives to England to plead their claims to the land, the appeal was lost. Many families went to Pennsylvania. Some stayed in Schoharie and others looked for land along the Mohawk River.

Catherine's family was among the 94 individuals who applied for Indian lands along the Mohawk River. As was the custom, buyers made a deal with the Native Americans and the Colonial Governor purchased the land from the Indians, had it surveyed and sold to the settlers. In 1723 Governor William Burnet was the Colonial Governor and honored the Palatines petition for 9,200 acres of land north and south of the Mohawk River between today's Little Falls and Frankfort. The document, known as the Burnetsfield Patent, was signed April 30, 1725 and Catherine was one of the 36 women given one hundred acres in her own name, unique in colonial documents.

Before 1722 Catherine had married Johan Jost Herkimer (1700-1775) who had come with his family from Germany. The marriage date is unknown but she is listed as Catherine Herkimer in the January 1723 petition for land and their oldest child Catherine was born in 1722.

Carving a homestead out of a forest (one tale was a squirrel could get from Buffalo to Albany without touching the ground) was a huge challenge, but, with neighbors working together, the settlement prospered. Again, Native Americans were of much help. Catherine and Johan Jost would have 13 children who lived to maturity; Gertrude (c1722-1806), Magdalena (1724-before 1817), Elizabeth Barbara (1726-1800), Nicholas (c1727-1777), Delia (1728-1804), Catherine (1729-after 1807), Hendrick (1730 – 1779), Elizabeth (c1733-1825), Johan Jost (1734-1795), Anna (1739- ?), George (1774-1788), Maria, and John (1745-1817). Two of the thirteen children had no children and there were 78 grandchildren and 365 great grandchildren.

Catherine's job was to have the children, prepare meals, see food and flax were grown, convert flax and sheep's wool into clothing, know enough about herbs to keep 15 people healthy, care for cattle and chickens to provide for the family and be principle teacher as the children grew. Her husband was the 2nd most powerful man in the area after Sir William Johnson. Johan Jost controlled 400 aces from the original Burnetsfield Patent (his father George's, his mother Magdalena's, his wife Catherine's and his own). He bought more land in 1748 (3,000 acres) and again in 1752 (2,000 acres). He was a successful farmer, grew

The home of Catherine and Johan Jost Herkimer built about 1740.

the grain, ran the mill that ground it and owned the boats that delivered supplies to the Fort at Oswego built in 1755.

Catherine and Johan Jost's first home was a log cabin but by the 1740s a two-story stone home with a basement and attic was lived in by the family. Their house was used as a trading post so Catherine would be in charge of running this when Johan Jost was away.

When the French and Indian War began in 1753 Catherine and Johan Jost Herkimer's home was fortified by the British Government. Walls were built around their stone house and the Fort Herkimer Church. At the time of enemy attacks, settlers would come to the fort for protection. The logistics of feeding and housing these other families as well as soldiers would be in Catherine's domain.

Catherine and Johan Jost died in 1775, both age 75. They did not suffer the heartbreak of having their family divided by loyalties. Oldest son Brigadier Nicholas Herkimer would organize and command the Tryon County Militia, trained to protect their frontier community. He would lead 700 members of the militia to support the Continential troops based at Fort Stanwix (today Rome, N.Y.). The Battle of Oriskany fought August 6, 1777 was part of the first civil war in the new nation. Daughter Elizabeth's husband Peter D. Schuyler, daughter Delia' husband Peter Bellinger, daughter Catherine's husband George H. Bell, fought under General Herkimer as well as his brothers Henry and George. However son Johan Jost Jr. fought on the side of the British at Oriskany as well as daughter Anna's husband Peter Ten Brock. Daughter Gertrude's husband Rudolph Shornaker and Elizabeth's husband Henrick/Henry Frey were sympathetic with the British. Daughter Maria's husband Abraham Rosencranz, the minister of the Fort Herkimer Church tried to stay neutral in these difficult times but the feeling at that time was, "those who were not with you were against you."

Nicholas would die of wounds received at Oriskany. His name would survive when the State of New York named the land taken from Montgomery County in 1791 after him. At that time the new Herkimer County was about one fifth of the State of New York and would eventually be subdivided into 14 Counties. Son Henry 's family settled around Schuyler Lake in Otsego County. Son George would inherit his brother Nicholas's property, which is today a New York State Historic Site. Son Johan Jost would settle in today's Kingston, Ontario, Canada owning a great deal of property there.

By the 1850 census of Herkimer County there were no persons named Herkimer living the county. However, many descendants of the eight daughters are still living in the county.

Catherine and her husband are buried in the Fort Herkimer Church Cemetery. No images or personal accounts of Catherine have been uncovered. Her legacy of courage, intelligence and skill have made her a woman worth remembering.

Jane Sullivan Spellman

MOLLY BRANT

was born about 1736 to Christian parents, Margaret and Cannassware. She was of the Wolf clan of the Mohawks and as a child lived in the Indian town of Canajoharie located on the Mohawk River about thirty miles upstream from Fort Hunter. Molly and her brother Joseph Brant (1743-1807) probably attended a school for children there and could read, write and speak Mohawk. She probably lived in one of the best houses in Canajoharie due to her mother's marriage to a Mohawk sachem. Molly also traveled to Philadelphia and other areas outside of Canajoharie with her stepfather, thus making her aware of English colonial life. The Mohawks maintained some of their traditions and beliefs but had adapted to some changes, which seemed to make their lives better.

Molly Brant was a Native American woman with many diverse qualities. She was sensible, handsome, judicious, mischievous, devout and respected.

Sir William Johnson (1715-1774), the most powerful man in upstate New York, was appointed Superintendent of Indian Affairs for the Northern District in 1756. He travelled all over the area and always stayed at the Brant home in Canajoharie while performing his duties there. He had taken a great interest in Molly's brother Joseph, sending him away to school and fostering his career. Sir William Johnson's wife, Catherine Weissenberg, the mother of their three children: Anne (born 1740), John (1741) and Mary (1744), died in the spring of 1759. That same year the first of Sir William and Molly's children Peter Warren was born (1759-1777). He was followed by Elizabeth (1763-1794), Magdalene (1765-1818), Margaret (1767-1844), George (1768-1822), Mary (1771- 1813), Susanna (1772-1785) and Anna (1773-1813). Their daughters married white men and had a total of 12 children. Neither son had children.

Sir William was 44 years old and Molly 24 when their first child was born. She helped Sir William keep important connections to the Mohawks. Even though Sir William and Molly were not married under British law, they lived together for fifteen years as husband and wife. She was in charge of a busy household and hostess to many important dignitaries such as New York governors, as well John Penn, Chief Justice of Pennsylvania and the Indian chiefs. Many Indian Councils were held at their home where treaties or land purchases were made. Molly often persuaded obstinate chiefs to agree to the terms of these decisions.

With Sir William Johnson's death in 1774, Molly and children moved to Canajoharie to live with her mother and family until 1777. She and her children left the region quickly after the Battle of Oriskany on August 6, 1777. Molly had sent information to brother, Joseph Brant, of the movements made by the Tryon County Militia on their way to assist the Contential troops at Fort Stanwix. This information helped the British prepare to ambush the militia.

With this sudden departure, many of her fine possessions and wealth were abandoned. Being Sir William's widow, she along with her brother, Joseph, were helpful in managing the destitute Indians at Fort Niagara making sure they received food and shelter from their British allies. These Indians had fled there ahead of the Sullivan-Clinton Campaign, which marched through the Finger Lake District destroying Indian villages. Only staying a few months at Niagara, Molly, some of her children and a group of Mohawks journeyed to live on Carleton Island at the head of the St. Lawrence River, near Cape Vincent, N.Y.

There was no mention of the Six Nations or protection of their right to native lands in the Peace Treaty of 1783 between the Americans and British. Molly had spent almost eight years helping the British retain support from the Iroquois. Her inheritance and that of her children was gone. Sometime later land in Canada was given to the Iroquois to replace what they lost.

In 1784 Molly moved to a fort at Cataraqui, Kingston, Ontario, Canada. Nearby brother Joseph had a home, although he lived mostly in a settlement north of Lake Erie. Her remaining years were spent being very active in the Anglican community of Kingston. Molly and son George were listed in 1792 as founders of St. Paul's Church in Kingston, Ontario.

Molly Brant portrayed on Canadian Stamp issued April 14, 1986 honoring her.

By living in Kingston, Molly was isolated from many other Iroquois. As a result she lost some of her influence among them.

Two of her daughters died a few years before she did. Molly died in Kingston on April 16, 1796 at her daughter Magdalene Ferguson's home. She is buried in the cemetery at St. Paul's Church but the exact spot of her grave is unknown.

There are no known portraits of her. In 1986 a Canadian postage stamp was issued in Molly's honor.

Susan Stevens Radell

SOPHIA DERBYSHIRE BAGG

was born September 25, 1778 in Hull, England, the daughter of Matthew Derbyshire who came to this country and settled in Hartwick in Otsego County. Earliest records of Sophia show her married to Moses Bagg, Jr. (1779-1844). Their first child daughter Emma was born September 15, 1813. Their son Moses Means was born July 13, 1816, Matthew Derbyshire on March 20, 1818 and Egbert born on February 2, 1820. Sophia's husband came to the Utica area with his father and mother, Moses Bagg, Sr. (1737-1805) and Elizabeth (c1740-1805) from Westfield, Mass. in 1793. Presumably, Moses and Sophia were married in Utica.

In 1814 on July 7, Sophia attended a revival meeting and joined the Presbyterian Church in Utica. This Church had been established in 1792 as the United Presbyterian Society of Whitestown and Old Fort Schuyler, the first Presbyterian Church west of Albany. In 1813, there was an amicable separation of the congregations as each congregation grew enough to support a minister. There were 57 people in the Utica Church and all Sophia's family except Matthew would join this church. Sophia was one of the women to organize the Oneida Female Missionary Society. This was the first woman's organization in the U.S. financially independent of the male dominated religious organizations. The women held offices of president, secretary, and treasurer. The Oneida was dropped from the Society's name but the Society continued to do missionary work both local and national.

Along with being a wife and mother, Sophia took an active part in running the Bagg's Hotel. Her father-in-law Moses Bagg, Sr. started the hotel in 1795 along with three other men. It was a two story wood structure. His son Moses, Jr. took over the tavern in 1808, built a three story brick hotel building between 1812-15 and the business prospered. Her son Moses Means wrote that Sophia held the weekly sewing circle,

Sophia Bagg lived in Bagg's Hotel built 1812-1815 on the site of Bagg's Tavern.

which raised money for her many charities, in the public rooms of the hotel. In 1824 Sophia and Moses built a big house with beautiful rooms, elaborate carvings and massive fireplaces where Sophia continued to hold her meetings of women who joined to create services needed in the growing community of Utica.

In June of 1824, Sophia became one of the founders of the Maternal Society, a group of women who gathered to learn about parenting and how to care for children. At that time, the church minister told mothers they should physically bring up their children but 'break their spirit', so when they came to the church they could be molded in the proper way. Needless to say, the women banded together to off set this weird idea. The Maternal Association became a national program and there was a national publication which started in Utica in 1833 and went all over the country

In 1825-26 The Female Missionary Society raised $192 to support a first revival given by the young charismatic Charles Grandison Finney (1792-1875). His message of salvation was achieved not merely by faith but also by good works. He felt slavery a sin. His message was so powerful and influential that an opposition group, the Oneida Association made up of a group of

Presbyterian ministers holding sentiments contrary to his, banded together to oppose his revivals. (It should be noted that Finney would have a church built in 1834 in New York City organized for him as he felt the world should be rid of intemperance, slavery, prostitution, profanity and all sin. He became the President of Oberlin College Ohio, the first co-educational college organized in 1836, as well as the Professor of Theology and Pastor of the Oberlin Community Church.)

While we have no names of women involved in the anti-slavery movement, it was following the Finney revival that the idea of new Oneida Institute of Science and Industry was proposed. Opened in May 1827, the school was to prepare young men for the Presbyterian ministry. It would be among the first of the work-study schools where students paid expenses by working. It also accepted black males. Its first President was Rev. George Washington Gale who would leave in 1834 to found Knox College. The 2nd president was Rev Beriah Greene (1795-1874) who presided at the first meeting of the American Anti Abolition Society in 1833 and brought the Anti Abolition Society to Utica in 1835. This Anti Abolition meeting was adjourned to Green's friend Garrit Smith's home in Peterboro because of the near riot in Utica.

In 1825 Sophia was one of the women to form the Female Society of Industry as well as in 1826 the Western Domestic Mission Society which lasted only two years. In 1828 she was part of the Society for the Care that held a large sewing bee that raised funds for her various charities including care of infants ages 18 months to two years. It took place in the parlor at the hotel where women gathered to sew and knit for others. One note said, "It went from Mrs. Bagg's sewing basket to $2,000 a year." This group hired a matron to look after three orphans and over the next 30 years, 750 children were cared for.

Sophia's four children all lived lives of giving to the community. Daughter Emma married Charles Addison Mann (1803-1860) a lawyer interested in real estate of the Holland Land Company. He served as the Oneida Bank President, President of the Utica Steam Cotton Mill and President of the N.Y., Albany and Buffalo Telegraph Co. and he was involved with the Utica and Schenect-ady Railroad. Charles was elected to the New York State Assembly in 1840 and elected to New York State Senate in 1850s. The Manns had five children, Sophia (1833-1870) married Alex Coventry, Charles Addison II (1835- 1896), a lawyer, James Ford (1837-1902), M.D., Matthew D. (1845-1921) M.D., and Emma (1847 -1910) married Joseph Swan a lawyer. Sophie would only know three of her grandchildren.

Second son Mathew Derbyshire, a graduate of Yale in 1839 and Harvard Law School practiced in Utica and New York City. Poor health brought him back to Utica. A bachelor, Matthew lived with his sister until his death. Third son Egbert a surveyor, distinguished himself during the Civil War retiring as a Lt. Col. He married Cornelia Hunt. He died at sea on his way to Europe on November 18, 1885 and was buried at sea. Their only son was the well-known ornithologist Egbert Bagg (1850-1915).

Sophia died September 19, 1832 at age 53. Sophia left no will.

Jane Sullivan Spellman

HARRIET DOUGLAS CRUGER

was born in New York City in 1790, the daughter of George and Margaret Corne Douglas. Her father was the third of four Douglas brothers who together established a successful business in London and New York City. George moved to New York City to operate the family business where the family made their residence.

George and Margaret Douglas had four daughters and two sons. When George died in 1799, Margaret, who was pregnant with their youngest child Betsy Mary (1799-1852), was left to bring up the children. The family would spend their summers at Henderson Cottage, built by Margaret in 1787 on the Herkimer County property that was originally bequeathed to Margaret's grandfather, Dr. James Henderson, by the English Royal Family as a land grant in 1739. Here, Harriet acquired a love for the property.

As a young woman, she accompanied her brother George (1792-1860) to Scotland where he attended Edinburgh University and Harriet had her first visit to her uncle, Sir William Douglas' residence called Gelston Castle. This visit made such an impression on her that she dreamed of one day building her own Scottish-style mansion. This dream would later lead to the construction of what was to be one of the most unique structures in Herkimer County.

While in Scotland, Harriet was placed in the charge of Mrs. Anne Grant of Laggan, who took in young ladies to "form their mind and manner." Mrs. Grant, a respected author in her own right, introduced Harriet into literary society, where she met the famous poets Sir Walter Scott and William Wordsworth. Most of her young life was spent traveling through Europe and America with one or more of her siblings where she moved in the best circles of society.

Sir Walter Scott even made mention of her in his journal: "Miss Douglas is a professed lion-huntress, who travels the country to rouse the peaceful beasts out of their lair and insists on being hand and glove with all the leonine race."

Her red-gold hair and lively manner made quite an impression everywhere she went. A book written about her life, by Angus Davidson (1953) best describes her - "Hers was a character of many contradictions and inconsistencies; it was generous and mean, selfish and self-sacrificing, pious and worldly; but it contained qualities which preserved it from mere ordinariness. There was in it a streak of originality."

After the death of her mother in 1830 and a year later, her eldest sister Margaret in 1831, Harriet decided to settle down and agreed to marry her on-again and off-again suitor Henry Nicholas Cruger (1800-1867), who was from one of the oldest and most distinguished families of New York. She married Henry in 1833 on the day of her birthday at the age of 43. He was 33.

Harriet Douglas from a portrait (1831) by Sir William Beechey, R.A.

From the beginning of their relationship, Harriet wanted Henry in the role of protector and counselor, but enjoyed holding the purse strings, among other things. Upon their marriage, she initially requested he take the Douglas name and they were known as Mr. and Mrs. Douglas Cruger. Harriet also retained control of her property and money in a marriage agreement, which was a cause of contention throughout their marriage.

They resided at 55 Broadway in New York where Cruger was a well-established lawyer. He continued in that profession until Harriet convinced him to devote himself to the management of the various Douglas estates, including the property in Herkimer County. About a year after their marriage, she had him undertake the project of building her castle summer home. The house, with its castle-like appearance, featured round bow windows, turrets, and castellated chimneys, with blocks of stone drawn up from Little Falls, and situated on a scenic spot, not far from the cottage her mother had built, overlooking the Mohawk Valley. According to an article "Landmark in Herkimer County Rich in Historic Interest," the castle contained upwards of 20 rooms, including eight bedrooms on the second floor, two on the first floor and three sitting rooms. A large hall also was used as a dining room. The basement had five rooms, a kitchen and a sitting room. There were numerous fireplaces throughout the structure. This structure was given the name of Gelston Castle.

Harriet loved her summers there entertaining visitors. Famed American novelist James Fennimore Cooper, who lived in nearby Cooperstown, was a friend of Harriet and Nicholas's, and was a regular visitor.

Their marriage only lasted eight years and may be described as a stormy one. Even though Harriet liked the security of a marriage, she was too independent to be "happily tied down." A family story was told that she had her marriage bed sawed in half and turned it into two unique sofas that were situated in the entrance way to the Castle House.

Their separation and the legal battles over the right to ownership of Harriet's property were headline news in the New York City newspapers. Henry eventually won half of Harriet's estate and lived out his life in Long Island, a wealthy man. Hendrik Hartog dedicates a chapter on their marital property dispute entitled "Coercion and Harriet Douglas Cruger" in his book *Man and Wife in America* (2000).

In 1850 at the age of 60, Harriet moved from 55 Broadway in New York City and built a new home at 128 West 14th Street. (In 1873 this house was rented by The Metropolitan Museum of Art to show their collection until their Central Park building was completed.) She still spent her summers in Herkimer County and invited the local children on Sundays to come there for Sunday school. Most of the servants were imported from Scotland and at the end of each summer; she would host a Harvest Home Festival with a particular Scottish flair.

In 1866 after a severe illness, Harriet began showing signs of mental upset. She was in fear for her soul and wished to leave her estates to religious uses. Continuing to decline in health, Harriet died at her house on West 14th Street on May 5, 1872.

She wished to be buried at her Henderson estate and even had an ornate stone sarcophagus made up for that purpose. The family instead had her buried in New York City and contested her will, which was rejected by the courts because "the testator having been of unsound mind" at the time she made it. Her Mohawk Valley estate was inherited by her niece Fanny Monroe (1824-1902) and her husband Douglas Robinson (1824-1893) and remained in the family until 1962 when Helen Roosevelt Robinson (1881-1962) was the last family member to reside there.

Only a shell of the castle structure remains to this day and some say that Harriet's spirit still roams the property she so loved in her lifetime.

Caryl Darling Hopson

SOPHRONIA FARRINGTON CONE

was born in Lynn, Massachusetts in 1802. She was just a babe in arms when she moved with her parents, Amos and Sara Upham Farrington from Lynn, Massachusetts to Herkimer County. They settled on high ground near the West Canada Creek and called it Farrington Hill (now Osborn Hill). It was there that Amos and Sara raised their ten children: John, Hannah, Sally, Amos, Jr., Henry, Sophronia, Mary (Polly), Pamelia, Harvey, and William. The family was industrious and charitable, followers of Englishman John Wesley, founder of the Methodist Church. Methodism came to America in 1769, its message spread by circuit-riding itinerant preachers up and down the east coast. Wesley was a firm believer in social justice, among the first to renounce slavery; it was said that to be a Methodist was to be an abolitionist. Wesley, who saw Methodism as a mission church said, "The world is our parish!"

And John Wesley spoke out to women. In an age when women had few, if any, rights, his ideas were unprecedented. He said, "You, like them, were made in the image of God. You are equal candidates for immortality. You too are called of God to do good unto all men. There is neither male nor female in Christ Jesus, you as well as men are rational creatures. Let all you that have it in your power, assert the right which the God of nature has given you. Be not disobedient to the heavenly calling. Whenever you have opportunity, do all the good you can."

Sophronia was intelligent, articulate and eager to learn. When the Methodist Church opened a co-educational, non-sectarian seminary in Cazenovia, NY, both she and her sister Pamelia enrolled and, in 1828, were two of the earliest graduates of the school that was to become Cazenovia College. After graduation Pamelia married and Sophronia taught in central New York and

Massachusetts schools. Five years later she learned of the death of Melville Cox in 1833, the first Methodist missionary to Liberia, a country founded in Africa by the American Colonization Society in 1821 to resettle free blacks. Already ill when he arrived, Cox died there just four months later of what they called "African fever." A plea went out for a replacement and

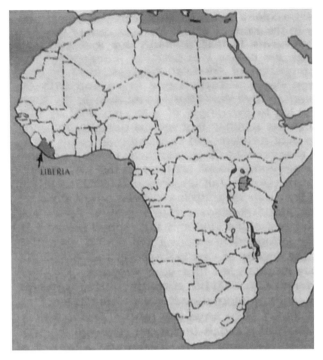

Map of Africa showing Liberia in black where Sophronia Farrington went as a missionary

Sophronia, moved by his death and John Wesley's words to women, offered to go. She was educated, devout and had a deep desire to serve. The Committee of the Boston Society probably had misgivings about sending the first unmarried female missionary to a foreign country, but they said she was anxious to go and 'her character was very fair'. She wouldn't go alone; two Methodist missionary couples from Massachusetts, Rev. Rufus and Nancy Jones Spaulding and Rev. Samuel and Phoebe Wiley Wright were also selected to go.

The ship, Jupiter, which had been provided by the ACS, left Norfolk on November 5, 1833 carrying seventy emigrant free blacks as well as the Methodist missionaries. The journey took 56 days, 'a lengthy but pleasant passage', although Sophronia said she was seasick every day. The voyage was made more pleasant by the attention of Captain Knapp who spared no pains to make their passage comfortable. Sophronia spent much of her time on deck where she entertained and instructed the emigrants with her drawings, paintings and stories. Many of them were educated and already Christian but others succumbed to her 'silvery voice' and were converted by the time the Jupiter arrived in Monrovia on New Year's Day 1834 where they were 'joyfully received'. Sophronia felt she had found her true calling.

In a letter to her friend, Miss Merritt, Sophronia described the natives thronging the streets to gaze at the foreigners. She found the area beautiful, the foliage, fruit and flowers lush and colorful, with shrubs, lofty oak and cotton trees, the sound of roaring surf and occasional thundershowers that cleared the air. She missed the privileges of America but said she had no regrets and had never felt more contented and happy any place. She wished simply for a comfortable bed, since she slept with only a pillow and a blanket.

They organized a Sunday school and Temperance Society and made plans to rebuild the Monrovia Church. A camp meeting in February was held 'in perfect order' for seven days. Sophronia saw a great need for schools, saying that some of the new emigrants wanted her to teach them, but she said, "My whole soul runs after the natives." It was said that "she charmed savages by her drawing and painting." Sophronia saw the people of Africa as a population awaiting the word of God but was appalled by their religious practices. As an example she said they carried offerings to a select man who was chosen to feed the Devil. In the evening he carried a bowl of palaver, a native dish, to Devil's Bush and in the morning when the bowl was found empty the people were made to believe the devil had eaten it and was therefore appeased. She asked Miss Merritt for "ardent, wrestling, mighty prayer for this benighted nation."

Within a short time African fever (probably malaria) took its toll on them all. Young Mrs. Phoebe Wright was only 23 when she died of fever in February. Samuel, her husband, followed her in a few weeks at the age of 25. The Spauldings and Sophronia became ill as well. The doctor gave up hope for Sophronia's recovery and withdrew her medicine. Amazingly, within two weeks, she was up again and writing. This is how she remembered her near-death experience:

"I felt alone and thought, Is there not someone here to sympathize with me? At once Jesus seemed to stand by my side and showed me that it was not His will that I should die at this time and that I should remain for the Mission's sake."

"I said, Then, Lord, remove the disease. Sudden as a flash of lightning the fever and pain all left me and I was well. The doctor said mine was the greatest cure he had ever wrought, to which I made no reply."

"Mr. Spaulding, our superintendent was to sail on the following Tuesday for America. He was calculating to take me with him and to give up the Mission. But I said, No, I can never see this Mission abandoned. I can die here but I will never return until the Mission is established."

"I said, I will stay and trust in the Lord."

The Spauldings returned to America in May without Sophronia. When missionary Dr. John Seys arrived in Monrovia on October 18th to take over the mission she greeted him, the last remaining white person in Monrovia. He described her as "a delicate, frail, emaciated woman who had braved all dangers for Christ's sake, had seen others die, but had not feared herself to die." She said, "I laid my life on the altar on leaving America and I am willing that it should remain there." Dr. Seys served as a missionary in Liberia for 25 years.

In April 1835 when she believed the mission was secure, Sophronia returned to America but never forgot those days in the field. Wherever she could she used her efforts to raise money for Africa and would gladly have returned as a missionary if she had been called. She returned to teaching and became guardian to a motherless teenage relative, Maruva Johnson. When she was fifty she married George Cone of Utica who was a grocer and a mover of buildings. Her large and devoted family and many friends called her "Aunt Sophronia Africa", a name she cherished. She passed away in 1880 and is buried in the Middleville Rural Cemetery behind the Methodist Church.

Family Notes on Sophronia, which were included in the Farrington genealogy state that she left no estate except for missions. It was necessary to sell her home to pay her debts and funeral expenses.

Joyce Fellows Murphy

MARY ANN BUELL MATHER

was born in 1805 in Fairfield, NY, a daughter of Roswell Buell (1772-1813) and Sarah Griswold Buell (1769-1856). Roswell Buell opened a store in the hamlet of Fairfield and donated an acre of land to the site of the Fairfield Academy which was erected in 1802. He also was a donor to the "Permanent Fund" dedicated to the fledgling school, which was to achieve prominence in the education of area youth. An epidemic swept the area known as the Royal Grant during the winter of 1812-1813 and Roswell fell victim to the disease, leaving his wife, son, and daughters.

Mary Ann was eight years old when her father passed away and the support of the family fell to brother, Alexander Hamilton Buell who was about 12 years of age. He went to work in a local store to support his mother and sisters while attending classes in his free time. Alexander eventually owned a store

Mary Ann Buell Mather's life centered around Fairfield Academy featured in the drawing. The old chapel on the right was built in 1802.

and expanded the mercantile business. An interest in politics led him to attain election to Congress in 1850 where he served until his early death in 1853.

Mary Ann grew up in the thriving community of Fairfield, a block away from the Fairfield Academy to which was added the College of Physicians and Surgeons of the Western District of New York in 1812. Life was exciting in a community filled with young people from other places aspiring to an academy education similar to high schools of today. The addition of young men seeking a medical education added to the social life of the village.

On May 24, 1836, Mary Ann married William Mather, M.D. at Trinity Episcopal Church in Fairfield. Dr. Mather (1802-1890) grew up around the corner from the Buell home and the families must have been closely associated during their childhoods as neighbors. Moses Mather, William's father, was a leader in the financing and building of the Academy. The young married couple moved into the Mather home directly across from the campus.

Dr. Mather did not practice medicine as he was not fond of that aspect of his education. His interest was chemistry. Two years after his marriage, he became an instructor of chemistry at Hamilton Literary and Theological Seminary. In 1841, he was professor of chemistry and pharmacy at Castleton Medical College in Vermont. From 1852-1868, he was professor of chemistry, geology, and mineralogy in Madison University (now Colgate). Lectures were a popular form of entertainment and Dr. Mather was on the lecture circuit throughout the state. Mary Ann was left alone much of the time while raising her three children and watching out for her widowed mother and mother-in-law. Letter writing was the only means of communication during the periods of separation. The three children grew up under the watchful eye of Mary Ann and the advice offered by their father during his absence.

The oldest child of Mary Ann was William Mather (1837-1908). Mary Ann was sometimes exasperated by "Willie" as her letters to his father reveal a son who sometimes did not do what was expected of him at home. William graduated from Fairfield Seminary in 1860. At the outbreak of the Civil War, he enlisted in a New Jersey regiment and achieved the rank of captain. Eventually he returned to Fairfield where the U.S. Census of 1870 listed him as a farm laborer. He was popular and in demand for his musical skills.

Mary Ann had a daughter, Martha Ann (1840-1927) who married Albert Barnes Watkins, a math teacher at the Seminary. When he advanced to serve as the Assistant Secretary of the Board of Regents from 1885-1892, he was frequently in Albany. Thus, Martha Ann resorted to letter writing as a means of keeping her family together on household issues.

The youngest member of Mary Ann's family was Alonzo Clark Mather (1848-1941). Surviving letters portray him as industrious and intelligent. His boyhood chores included carrying wood for the stove that warmed Trinity Church for morning services. He left home to seek his fortune in the city of Utica. After moving to Chicago he invented a stock car (1881) for shipping cattle to market in a humane manner. Eventually he built the 42-story Mather Tower in Chicago and the 10-story Mather Building in Washington, DC.

Mary Ann wrote her son many letters as his fortune rose, but she did not live to see his ultimate fame. She passed away on November 8, 1874, and was buried in Trinity Churchyard with the Mathers and Buells. She was a woman who did the best she could in her roles of wife and mother during the stress of the Civil War and her husband's career demands. Dr. Mather survived her by sixteen years, leaving a variety of papers and letters as well as his writings of historical importance.

Jane Winterbottom Dieffenbacher

ELIZA HART SPALDING

was born August 11, 1807 the oldest of the six children of Levi and Martha Hart. Her sisters were Lorena and Caroline and brothers Zenas, Cyrus and Horace. The family moved to Holland Patent in 1820 from Kensington, Conn. Although the family was not particularly religious, Eliza appeared before a session of the Presbyterian Church in Holland Patent on August 26, 1826 and was officially received in the Church. Her family chose to send her to The Clinton Academy in Clinton instead of the much closer Fairfield Academy perhaps for religious reasons.

A mutual friend suggested Eliza correspond with Henry Harmon Spalding (1803-1874), a man interested in missionary work. For over a year they exchanged letters and they met in 1831 when Henry visited Holland Patent. He was enrolled in the Western Reserve College in Huron, Ohio for his last two years of college and convinced Eliza's parents to send Eliza to a girls' school there. Henry graduated from Western Reserve on August 28, 1833 and he and Eliza were married October 13, 1833. They went to Cincinnati so Henry could enter the new Lane Theological Seminary where both attended lectures by Dr. Lyman Beecher, the new president of the seminary. Perhaps Eliza met his daughter Harriet, who was four years her junior. Harriet would marry Calvin Stowe in 1836 and write Uncle Tom's Cabin in 1852.

During his two years of school, Henry applied for missionary work under a government program. Not hearing from them Henry reapplied to the American Board of Commissioners for Foreign Missions, an organization formed in 1812, based in Boston by Congregational, Presbyterian and Dutch Reformed Churches who worked together to supply missionaries where needed. He was given permission to go to the Osage Indians in West Missouri. In a long letter of recommendation was the sentence "His (Henry's) wife is very highly respected and beloved by a large circle of friends on Walnut Hill and in Cincinnati. She is one of the best women for a missionary wife with whom I am acquainted".

The Spaldings suffered the loss of a stillborn daughter in October of 1835, but it made it possible for them to accept an offer from Marcus Whitman, M.D. (1802-1847) to join him and his wife Narcissa Prentiss (1808-1847) Whitman on their mission to the western Indians. On March 31, 1836, after fundraising to get supplies and money for the trip, the Spaldings and Whitmans left Liberty, Mo. with the American Trade Caravan headed for the Rocky Mountains. The two couples were among the 10 people, 17 head of cattle including four milk cows and two calves, twelve horses and six mules at the end of the caravan. They arrived in Laramie, Wyoming the end of June. When they arrived at Fort Walla Walla on September 12, they were treated to the first amenities since leaving Liberty. Eliza and Narcissa were the first white women to cross the Continental Divide at South Pass, Wyo.

By September, Henry Spalding and Marcus Whitman decided their strong personalities would not let them work in the same place. The Whitmans stayed on the Walla Walla River among the Cayuse Indians and the Spaldings went 100 miles to Lapwai amid the Nez Perce tribe. In the 1830 there were about 6,000 members of this tribe who had sent representatives to St. Louis to ask for missionary help.

Eliza arrived at the site chosen by Henry and the Indians on November 29, 1836, and in her diary wrote: "Yesterday reached this desirable spot, where we expect to dwell the remnant of our earthly pilgrimage. As yet our dwelling is an Indian Lodge, which must serve us some time for there is no preparation for building yet. Blessed be God that we have been spared to accomplish a long & tedious journey…"

The Spaldings lived in the lodge of buffalo hides for three weeks while Henry, assisted by the willing hands of the Indians, built a log house forty two by eighteen feet: eighteen feet at one end was living quarters and the rest for mission purposes. This was the first white settlement in what is now Idaho.

Eliza went to work, learning from the Indian women much about living in the wilderness. The Nez Perce bought food including fresh trout which was salted for winter use. Eliza was good at languages and began to learn the Nez Perce language and put the Bible into the Nez Perce language. Her skill at painting was used to tell Bible stories in the school she established January 27, 1837. She was able to teach the young girls weaving and sewing skills. While Henry was busy constructing buildings, dams and mills, Eliza was building a friendly atmosphere where all were welcome. The first two years they had some visitors but Eliza and Henry were the only white settlers.

Henry felt he had to help the Nez Perce Indians learn how to cultivate crops so they could settle in one place to learn about God. The tribesmen were hunters and had to travel many miles to get the elk, deer, buffalo, which supported their families. Henry was criticized for putting the building first and not the preaching, but it would be the Spaldings who had the first baptisms and developed a lasting relationship with the Indians.

Eliza Spalding lived in this mission. Photo was taken in 1890 with upper portions removed from building erected in 1838.

Henry also built a second home, this one two stories, 32'x22' in time for the arrival of daughter Eliza on November 15, 1838. She was the first white child born in Idaho and first white child to live to maturity in the Oregon territory. She added to her Mother's busy schedule. Son, Henry Hunt arrived on November 24, 1839, daughter, Martha Jane, March 20, 1845, and Amelia Lorene, December 12, 1846.

When he left on March 17, 1837 to get supplies at the Hudson Bay store, Henry left Eliza with 1,500 Indians settled nearby. Henry returned with several hoes and with the Indian help, was able to put 100 acres under cultivation.

By 1838 seven more white people came to the mission. The three additional men helped to build a blacksmith shop, a bigger school and a mill race. There were now 100 Indian families planting crops, sending their children to school and attending Sunday services. With the arrival of a printing press, books for the children were printed in their own language.

Letters by Eliza and Henry sent back east were full of success stories yet always asked for help. Eliza's church in Holland Patent filled several barrels of clothing to send and the story of what was happening was published in missionary magazines and the national press.

In 1840 there was some petty bickering among the two missions. A conference was called with the result being a Presbyterian Church established with officers to make judgments on behavior. There were three baptisms of Indians all from the Spalding mission.

People were coming West: 1,000 in 1842 and 10,000 in 1843. These travelers had a big impact on the mission. Not only did the newcomers expect welcome and help but the growing numbers made the Indians hostile as their land was taken over. In 1847 an outbreak of measles brought by the newcomers caused many Indian children to die. Eliza also contacted the measles and was at death's door for several weeks. The Indians would not accept Dr. Whitman's medicine and several Indian leaders began to feel the white man's way of life, no drinking, no gambling or limiting the number of wives, was not the way for them.

The American Board of Missions ended their financial support of the Spalding's mission in 1842 since the settlement was self - supporting. With the massacre at Waiilatpu led by the Cayuse Indians on November 29, 1847 and the murder of Narcissa and Marcus Whitman with 12 others along with 47 taken as prisoners, all other support ended.

Eliza heard the news of the massacre, and since Henry was returning from taking daughter Eliza to Waiilatpu for school, had no news of his safety. The Nez Perce Indians surrounded Eliza to protect their well-loved lady until Henry returned. He moved the family to the Willamette Valley to have their home nearer a fort's protection. Henry would continue to work for establishing the Oregon Territory in 1848. The new territorial governor sent Eliza, the oldest white woman in the territory, a rocking chair.

Eliza never regained her health after the birth of Amelia in 1846 and the tragic massacre in 1847. She survived until January 7, 1851, age 43, her youngest daughter only 4 years old. Eliza was buried in Brownsville, Oregon. In 1913 her remains were moved to be placed next to her husband's who died August 3, 1874 at Lapwai near Lewiston, Idaho. In 1936 the site was part of an Idaho state park and it is included in Nez Perce National Historical Park created in 1965.

Jane Sullivan Spellman

AMY BARBER ARNOLD

was born in Massachusetts on June 22, 1808, the daughter of John Calvin Barber and Elizabeth Doud Barber. Shortly after her birth, John Calvin and Elizabeth brought Amy and three older siblings, Calvin, Luther, and Eunice to Montgomery County, N.Y. Another daughter, Freelove Barber, was born there in 1810 followed by four more children during the next decade; Julia Ann, John C., Jr., Phebe, and Nathaniel B. Barber. The John C. Barber family was listed in the 1820 Federal Census for Newport, Herkimer County but moved to a farm near Whitestown in Oneida County by 1823 according to family historians.

Although Amy obtained a rudimentary common school education, she spent most of her time learning domestic skills to prepare for her role as a wife and mother. In 1827, at age 19, she married twenty-three year old Otis Nathaniel Arnold who was born in Dudley, Massachusetts and worked on a neighbor's farm near the Barber family. For several years Otis and Amy scraped out a living on a small farm in the Town of Boonville in Northern Oneida County. Here Amy gave birth to seven children in rapid succession; an infant that died in 1828, then Edwin, Almira Eliza, Harriet Almeda, Amy Diantha, Eunice, and Ophelia who arrived in 1836.

Amy Arnold's family lived in this house built in 1814, abandoned and occupied by Arnold's in 1838.

Otis struggled to make their farm productive. On a trip into Brown's Tract, a vast wilderness region northeast of Boonville in Northern Herkimer County, he discovered an abandoned dwelling that was built in 1814 by Charles Frederick Herreshoff during a failed attempt to mine iron ore in Brown's Tract. The dwelling, called the Manor House, an old forge and mill, and several barns at the foot of the Fulton Chain of Lakes, were owned by descendents of the original land speculator, John Brown of Providence, Rhode Island. Without benefit of a deed, Otis decided in 1837 to move his family deep into the North Woods beyond the reach of landlords and tax collectors.

The laborious journey, driving a few head of livestock along the rugged, twenty-five mile trail into the Tract covered by dense forests, streams and bogs, and huge boulders, took the Arnold family three days. Amy set up housekeeping in the spacious, hillside Manor House while Otis planted a few crops in the cleared fields that lay below along the Moose River. In exchange for more space for her growing family, Amy had forsaken the convenience of village shops, schools for her children, church services and socials, and most importantly, the companionship of her sister Julia Ann who also lived in Boonville since her marriage in December 1829 to Ephraim Bullock.

Amy Barber-Arnold gave birth to another daughter, Joanna, in July 1839 and twin daughters, Dolly and Julia, in April of 1941. Three more children were born over the next five years in Brown's Tract, all without benefit of a doctor; Esther in November 1842, Otis Jr. in June 1845, and Elizabeth in May 1847.

The Moose River region and Fulton Chain of eight lakes connected by portages drew a seasonal sortie of hunters, trappers and fishermen. Brown's Tract sojourners, astonished to find a family with twelve children living deep in the remote wilderness, began knocking on the Arnold's door seeking food and shelter. Otis started providing pack horses for the trek into the Tract, boats for the fishermen, and guiding services for the sportsmen.

Amy Arnold served up loaves of bread and stacks of pancakes with fresh churned butter and homemade jams, platters of venison, game birds, and pan-fried trout for their guests. When her husband was off hunting, trapping, or guiding for days, she supervised the planting and harvesting of farm crops and the care of the livestock. Guests were never turned away, and she often had to rise in the middle of the night to prepare a meal for a weary traveler.

News of Arnold's place in Brown's Tract spread and the hostelry at "Arnold's Clearing" was subsequently noted as a traveler's destination in several Adirondack guidebooks, newspaper articles, periodicals, and on 19th Century maps of Northern New York State. In 1849, an author, Joel T. Headley, wrote:

> *"The agricultural part is performed mostly by the females who plow, sow, rake, bind, &c equal to any farmer. Two of the girls threshed alone with common flails five hundred bushels of oats in one winter while their father and brother were away trapping for marten. These girls ride horses with a wildness and recklessness that makes one tremble for their safety."*

> *Headley went on to write that the Arnold daughters rode "with their hair streaming in the wind, and dresses flying about their white limbs and bare feet, careering across the plains, they look wild and spirited enough for Amazons . . . Yet they are modest and retiring in their manners, and mild and timid as fawns among strangers. The mother, however, is the queen of all woodmen's wives but you must see her and hear her talk to appreciate her character."*

Otis and Amy Arnold and eight of their children were still the only residents living in Brown's Tract, Northern Herkimer County according to the 1850 State Census. Although Otis and Amy could read and write, the decision was made to board several of their daughters outside of the Tract to further their education. The eldest daughter Almira married a widowed farmer, Moses Lyman Baldwin in 1849 and moved to Marcy, near Utica, N.Y. Her 16-year-old sister Amy went along to attend school. To raise twelve children to adulthood in the mid-1800s as Amy Arnold did was extraordinary. Of the four children her daughter Almira Baldwin gave birth to between 1853-1859, only one child survived.

Four more daughters married during the 1850s and left the Tract. Otis was able to raise a large quantity of oats yearly, which he drew on sleighs to market in Boonville during the winter. Severe winter storms and temperatures as low as minus 40 degrees kept the family housebound for months at a time without mail or newspapers from the world beyond the Tract. Spring through autumn brought scores of guests to the Manor House including the first female visitors. In September 1855, Governor Horatio Seymour arrived with his niece and the Honorable Amelia Murray, a maid of honor to Queen Victoria. The event so startled the six Arnold daughters still at home that it rendered them speechless.

Thomas B. Thorpe, after an 1858 visit to Arnold's Clearing, wrote in Harpers New Monthly Magazine:

> *"The mother was justly proud of the twelve children she had reared in her solitary home. Not a physician had ever crossed her threshold and yet they were pictures of health . . . All this was the result of a mother's care. Truly Mrs. Arnold is a model of her sex."*

By 1860, the census taker recorded eleven residents in Brown's Tract: eight members of the Arnold family plus three bachelor hunters who had taken up residence along the lakes. One of the bachelors, Sam Dunakin, left in the spring of 1861 to enlist as a sharpshooter in the Union Army. The Arnold boys, Edwin and Otis Jr., remained in Brown's Tract to help their aging parents support the family. Amy Arnold suffered the tragic news in April of 1863 that her daughter Almira Baldwin had died in Iowa at the age of thirty-two not long after she had given birth to two more children.

Traveling into the Tract was still a grueling journey in the 1860s over the primitive Brown's Tract road from the westward towns of Boonville or Port Leyden. Buckboards and pack horses were available only during the warm months but most travelers found it safer to dismount and traverse the trail on foot. Amy Arnold longed to see her grandchildren but only one married daughter, Ophelia, lived within twenty-miles at Raquette Lake with her husband Alonzo Wood and baby boy Alfred.

Three decades at her outpost in Brown's Tract tending to the needs of twelve children and providing hospitality to hundreds of wilderness travelers took its toll on Amy Arnold's health. In early April of 1868, Otis Jr. hastened out on the twenty-five mile trek to Boonville to fetch a doctor for his mother who was feeling "very low." The last few weeks of her life were spent among her loved ones at her Manor House in Arnold's Clearing where she died on June 22, 1868. Amy's body was carried out of the Tract to Boonville, Oneida County, NY for burial in the local cemetery.

Three of Amy Arnold's children continued the Arnold tradition of providing hospitality to wilderness travelers in Brown's Tract. Otis Arnold Jr. formally leased the Manor House for several years but died of consumption in 1883 in Brown's Tract. Until his death in 1906, Edwin Arnold took in lodgers at his small camps on Fourth Lake and Seventh Lake and guided sportsmen. Ophelia Arnold-Wood, known fondly as "Grandma Wood," and her husband Alonzo successfully operated Wood's Camp on the North Shore of Fourth Lake for three decades.

The origin of tourism, the life-blood of the economy for the Old Forge-Fulton Chain of Lakes region today, is rooted in the hard labors and legacy of this historic family led by its matriarch Amy Barber-Arnold. As author Joseph Grady wrote in 1938, *"They deserve to be remembered, above all, as a sturdy family of Adirondack pioneers who kept the fires of the Fulton Chain burning—when no one else would."*

Peg Nash Masters

.

HANNAH AVERY DEVEREUX KERNAN

was born in Utica on September 20, 1820, the first of Nicholas (1791-1855) and Mary Dolbeare Butler (1797-1880) Devereux's six children. Her father had come from Ireland to Utica in 1806, age 16 and joined his brother John, 17 years his senior, in a very successful store. Nicholas became involved with the store, bank, railroads and buildings with his brother and they founded St. John's Catholic Church, Utica, the first Catholic Church west of Albany, N.Y. in 1819. Hannah's parents were married November 28, 1817 in New York City. Nicholas and Mary

Hannah Avery Kernan at age 81 taken c. 1901

Devereux had six children: Hannah, John C. (1823), Catherine (1825), Mary (1828), Cornelia (1831) and Thomas (1833). There was considerable wealth in both her father and mother's families and she grew up in large homes in Utica.

At age 10 Hannah was sent to her Butler grandparents in New York City to attend Madame Binsse de St. Victoire School. Her grandfather Dr. Benjamin Butler was an MD but also a Wall Street broker who was influential in New York life. Hannah's father Nicholas visited her four or five times a year when he was in New York City buying goods for the Utica store. Hannah would return to Utica in 1838, age 18, "finished." That fall she was hostess at a party for 80 with only one married couple so there seems to have been many young people around. She probably met Francis Kernan (1816-1892) at church soon after his arrival in Utica in 1839 to begin the practice of law.

Francis Kernan was born January 4, 1816 in Tryone, Steuben County oldest son of the 10 children of William (1781-1870) and Roseanna Marie Stubbs (1789-1862) Kernan. He attended local schools and went to Georgetown University in Washington, D.C. in 1833 where his mother's brother Edward Stubbs was a successful businessman. After three years Francis returned home to study law with his sister Margaret's husband Edward Quinn in Watkins Glen, N.Y. He would move to Utica in May 1839 to join the Joshua Spencer Law Firm. Francis passed the NYS Bar in 1840.

Hannah and Francis were engaged in February 1843 and their marriage took place on May 23, 1843 at St John's Church: Hannah was 22 and Francis 27. Of note: the wedding ceremony was to be just family but when the couple arrived at church there were 1,500 people there. The planned reception was held the next day for invited guests.

Their first child John Devereux Kernan was born in 1844, Nicholas in 1845, Mary Agnes in 1847, Rosanna in 1849, Elizabeth in 1851, Francis Jr. in 1853, Thomas in 1856, William in 1858, Joseph in 1861 and Walter in 1864. Seven boys and three girls in 20 years made for a very large family. When you consider all the baptisms, first days at school, confirmations as well as birthday celebrations, there was always a great deal of activity in that household. Since Francis came from a family of 10, and many members moved from Francis' birthplace in Schuyler County to Utica, there was also a very large extended family.

During these early years, Francis was developing his law practice. In 1853 Francis opened his own office with his sister Winifred's husband, George Edward Quinn as a partner. That same year he was appointed to a state job as reporter for the NYS Court of Appeals. In this job he studied briefs, arguments and opinions of the judges in each case to prepare for a summary of each case for publication. During the 2 ½ years he was away in this position he wrote to Hannah daily. Hannah was left to run the busy household.

In 1860 Francis won a NYS Assembly seat serving for 1861-62. He was elected to Congress 1863-64 as well as elected Regent of the State University of NY 1870-1892. He was appointed United States Senator from 1876-1882. Francis' youngerbrother William lived at the home at 2 Kent Street while attending school, and would join his brother's law firm in 1857.

Hannah had her hands full with their 10 children and in 1857 Francis parents, William and Rosanna Stubbs Kernan, moved from Steuben County to Utica as did four of their children and their families.

Hannah lost her father Nicholas Devereux on December 28, 1855 at age 64. Helping her mother to cope with her father's large estate was part of her responsibilities. Husband Francis was the estate's attorney, which helped. The year before Nicholas died, he had traveled to Italy with his wife and daughter Mary to encourage a Franciscan Order to come to the U.S. to start a college. He had purchased from the Holland Land Company 400,000 acres of land in Allegany and Cattaraugus County and gave the Franciscan Fathers the land to build what would become St. Bonaventure College. Nicholas also gave and raised money to establish the American College in Rome, Italy. His widow would carry out his many plans after his death.

In 1861 Francis was Chairman of the NY State Democratic Convention in Syracuse and the New York Times carried his entire speech. The Civil War posed a real problem because Francis believed the South should correct their own slavery issue, yet when war was declared Francis felt the Union was more important. However, sons John D. and Nicholas were not sent to Georgetown University where their father had studied, but to the new (1856) Seton Hall College in NJ which would be safer than the Washington, D.C. area. The other five sons did attend Georgetown University after the Civil War ended.

While Francis worked long days and was gone a lot, Hannah kept the family together. In 1867, their daughter Mary Agnes (age 20) left to join the Sisters of Charity convent in Albany. Sadly, she died in 1870, the first of their ten children to die. That year son Thomas began studying for the priesthood although he had to leave his studies due to poor health. That same year Francis's father William Kernan died.

The first wedding in 1871 was of second son Nicholas to Harriet Ann Jenkins of Baltimore, MD. at an impressive ceremony in Baltimore attended by Cardinal Gibbons. This couple had 13 children and lived in the home on 3 Rutgers Park built by noted architect Phillip Hooker.

In 1873, two weddings took place: Roseanna to Thomas McCarthy of Syracuse in April, which ended sadly when Roseanna died the next year. First son John D. married Katherine Peebles in New Castle, PA. John had joined his father in the Kernan and Quinn firm. He and Katherine would have six children.

A large tribute to Hannah's reputation as a gracious hostess was when President Grover Cleveland came to Utica in July 1887 with his new bride, Frances Cleveland. They spent the night at the Kernans' before visiting his sister Rose in Holland Patent.

Frances spent the year before he died living quietly in his home. Hannah was with him in daily visits to church just a few blocks away. His death September 7, 1892 at age 78 was honored by his large funeral. Hannah would survive him by 10 years dying September 30, 1902. She and Francis are buried in St. Agnes Cemetery in Utica.

Her will left her considerable estate to her 8 surviving children: her only surviving daughter "Liz: was given all her personal effects, leaving a trust for son Thomas."

Creating a comfortable living environment for a nationally involved husband and children, who gave of themselves to their community, is powerful legacy. Hannah saw a great example in her parents and grandparents and used her education and financial advantages to make a difference in the world around her.

Jane Sullivan Spellman

HELEN ELIZABETH MUNSON WILLIAMS

was born August 28, 1824 the daughter of Alfred (1793-1854) and Elizabeth (1798-1870) Munson. They came to Utica shortly after their marriage in 1823, and amassed the family wealth through lucrative investments in burgeoning industrialization and developing transportation systems. Helen began her formal education at a dame's school at age three-and-a-half and at age twelve enrolled in the Utica Female Academy, where the curriculum included Algebra, Geometry, French, Physics, Logic, and Latin. When she was a teenager, her father took her on trips to Baltimore, where he had an iron works, and to New York, Philadelphia, and Washington. These uncommon parental influences—in depth education, domestic travel at a time of early industrialization, and an intimate knowledge of her father's successful business ventures—situated Helen to follow an uncommon path later in life.

In 1846, after a romantic courtship, Helen married Utica attorney James Watson Williams (1810-1873), who became an aide to his entrepreneurial father-in-law assisting with business affairs, acting as an investor, a legal advisor, and a lobbyist at sessions of the state legislature. Helen and James had three daughters, Grace (1847-1854), Rachael (1853-1915) and Maria (1853-1936). A steadfast moral and religious philosophy was an abiding influence on Helen as she guided her daughters in their character formation. She used her talent for writing poetry to gently instruct them and to cultivate the desired habits of behavior. A sixty-line poem written from a New York City hotel to her five-year-old daughter Rachel, for example, displays Helen's parental affection and long-distance tutelage. A four-verse poem unambiguously points Rachel and Maria on a spiritual path and ends with specific deportments and lessons addressed to each daughter.

When James' business dealings required him to travel—and they often did—he wrote sentimental, romantic letters to his wife and affectionate, fatherly messages to his daughters. Helen's Valentine poems to James—and his letters to her—project an amorous, impassioned relationship between them. Nineteenth-century conventions of behavior would not have sanctioned a public display of these emotions, but, privately, they were free to express their strong, romantic sentiments. James seems to have preferred gentlemanly scholarship over business affairs. He treated his debtors with such leniency that he was left without funds to pay his own creditors. In comparing her husband with her father, Helen wrote, "Two men more unlike in their tastes and habits, it might have seemed, could hardly have been associated so intimately together."

After a few years of marriage, the couple engaged Albany, N.Y., architect William Woolette (1815-1874) to design an Italianate-style home for them. Helen and James were actively involved in the planning of their cherished Genesee Street home, later called Fountain Elms. A gift from Helen's father, the state-of-the-art home featured a furnace and indoor bathroom when completed in 1852. The couple decorated their new home in the popular rococo revival style, patronizing preeminent New York City cabinetmakers such as Charles Baudouine. A group of family portraits and a collection of sculpture—the modest beginnings of what would become a significant art collection—complemented their furniture selections.

As the mistress in her household, Helen dispensed "parental" oversight and moral guardianship to the family's servants, with explicit regulation of working time, duties to be performed, and manner of dress and personal grooming. Helen's "Daily Duties" for her cook begin with these pronouncements, "Rise at 6 o'clock. Dress neatly in all respects; and in particularly never go into the kitchen without a tidy head." Leisure activities and, oftentimes, more intimate aspects of a servant's life also came under the mistress's scrutiny and direction. She exercised her privilege to claim an employee's availability with this understanding: "To consider that the engagement is for his time for anything that may be required within or without working hours...."

The deaths of Helen's parents and her only sibling (Samuel Munson, 1826-1881), who also possessed considerable wealth, positioned her as the sole manager of the Munson assets. In 1883 the New York Sun described her as the "richest person in Utica." A well-educated woman, at a time when education for girls was limited, Helen assumed the traditional domestic responsibilities of a nineteenth-century woman, but she also moved with apparent ease into unconventional roles of financial manager, investor, and philanthropist. Under her judicious guidance, the family fortune was markedly enhanced.

After James Williams' death in 1873, Helen and her two daughters, Rachel and Maria, adopted a more affluent lifestyle. Increased domestic and international travel and a heightened awareness of trend-setting families in larger cities influenced the ensuing choices made by the Williams women. Commencing in 1876 Helen and her daughters refurbished the interior of Fountain Elms, working with firms such as Pottier and Stymus, and Herter Brothers, the most fashionable cabinetmakers and interior decorators of the time. In addition, Helen sought to refine the home's interior decor with an extensive collection of fine Asian ceramics, exceptional decorative arts, and American and European paintings. An examination of her painting collection provides an insightful glimpse into the broader social and historical influences on Victorian collectors.

Advice from her friend and artist Henry Darby, the knowledge she gleaned from travel, exposure to well-known art collections of wealthy individuals, and the guidance she received from owners of the recognized New York City art galleries she patronized influenced Helen's fine art selections. Helen worked with some of the most esteemed galleries of the period, including Daniel Cottier and M. Knoedler. She was not enamored of avant-garde artists and disregarded the spontaneous brushstrokes and high-colored palettes of Impressionists. Instead, she turned her attention to fashionable painters of the Barbizon School who depicted sentimentalized images of peasants and rural settings, selecting paintings by Jean-Baptiste-Camille Corot, Paul Signac, Leon J. F. Bonat, Jules Dupré, and Jean-François Millet among others. Helen also favored the ideal landscapes of American artists from the Hudson River School, such as Frederic Edwin Church, Sanford Gifford, and William Hart. These stunning canvases appealed to her personal values and were consistent with her home's fashionable, yet conservative, interior decor.

Paintings, important decorative elements in a home, are also reflective of the personality of the owner. Helen's selections—with themes of family, domesticity, and devotion—may have been prompted by the contemporary acceptance of these topics or, perhaps, by the deeply melancholic aspects of her own life. Diary entries indicate that, in spite of attentive care, the Williams's first child, Grace, died unexpectedly at age seven. Helen's grief is succinctly stated, "...her hands and arms were cold. She was dying & we knew it not." Much later, Helen prepared for the birth of her first and only grandchild, but daughter Maria's child did not survive.

Helen seems to have acquired fine art for two main reasons: first, it met with her artistic sensibilities on a purely aesthetic level and was in accord with the mood she thought suitable for Fountain Elms, and, second, collecting works of fine art was considered to be an appropriate activity for a woman of her stature and she hoped her collection would also prove a future asset. In the upstate New York region,

Helen Munson portrait by Frederick Spencer done in 1843 before her marriage.

Helen set a standard among her peers for art acquisitions. Satisfied that her purchases were good investments, artistically and monetarily, Helen spent considerable funds to obtain them. Helen's art collection and the effects of many of her decisions remain as legacies not only for this community, but also for a wider realm. She believed in the importance of the arts for the edification of the community and that authentic experiences with art inspire, reveal insights, and foster creativity.

Helen's collecting habits were only outdone by her philanthropy. Although Helen was a meticulous account manager, keeping track of every penny, she was magnanimous. Her generosity extended to individuals who appealed to her directly and to multiple causes for the poor and less fortunate. Helen helped finance the building of a new City Hall, the renovations of Grace Episcopal Church, and the building to house the county Historical Society. She also assisted in the establishment of the House of the Good Shepherd.

Helen died in 1894 without a generation of heirs to follow her daughters. The Utica Herald quoted an acquaintance's description, ". . . I should call her a very charitable woman. She was a remarkably conscientious and religious woman, and of great cultivation of mind. She read much and had a discriminating taste."

Daughters Rachel and Maria Williams Proctor followed in their parent's footsteps. As young girls, Helen encouraged them to donate part of their allowances to charity. As adults, they carried this practice forward. Helen instilled in her daughters the importance of dedication to the community. Rachel and Maria inherited the collection established by their mother. They and their husbands, Frederick and Thomas Proctor, respectively, added significant paintings and smaller works of art. It was, however, Helen Munson Williams's keen aesthetic eye that set in motion the intentional selection of decorative and fine arts that led to the establishment of what is today the Munson-Williams-Proctor Arts Institute, Utica. MWPAI is dedicated to enriching the lives of the community and beyond by building on the initial art collection and resources provided by Helen's legacy. It remains Utica's greatest cultural asset.

Anna Tobin D'Ambrosio

MARTINA LOUISE
CONDICT BRANDEGEE

was born February 8,1826 in Morristown N.J., the youngest daughter of Dr. Louis Condict (1772-1862) and Martina Elmendorf (1784-1851) Condict. Martina's father was a prominent doctor, organizer and first president of the New Jersey State Medical Society, a US Congressman, a businessman and a trustee of Princeton College for 40 years. He and his first wife had ten children, most of them out of the house when Dr. Condict married Martina Elmendorf in 1824. Martina Louise grew up in a lovely 1797 Federal style house her father built that is today owned by the Women's Club of Morristown, N.J. and is part of the historical tour of that city.

Martina attended schools in Bethlehem, PA. On June 1, 1851, Martina married the Rev. John Jacob Brandegee, D.D. (1823-1864) in Morristown, N.J., moving with him to Litchfield, CT. before coming to Utica in 1854 when John was named pastor of Grace Episcopal Church. This congregation began in 1838 with members from Trinity Church, organized in 1798. Among the founders of Grace Church was Alfred Munson who worked with well-known architect, Robert Upjohn to design the new church. The cornerstone was laid in 1856 and in 1860 the beautiful new Grace Church on the corner of Genesee and Elizabeth Street was dedicated. It may have been the strain of raising the money and getting the church built in record time or an illness that caused her husband's death on April 6, 1864 at age 41, leaving Martina to find a new home to raise their four children.

Martina Louise moved her family from the parish house to the corner of Kent and Elizabeth Streets, one of the big houses around Chancellor Square where the children had playmates among the 'first families' of Utica. Oldest son John Elmendorf Brandegee, born July 9, 1853 in New London, CT., graduated from Utica Free Academy in 1870, from Trinity College in 1874 and Columbia Law School in 1876 and came back to practice law in Utica. His contributions to Utica were so numerous that a new school opening in 1911 was named after him. John never married, lived with his mother and only survived her by one year when he died in 1905 at age 51. John's hand written will left money to his mother and sister but he specified none of his money was to be used for religious projects. He wanted no fuss at his funeral, no music, no sermon. He left a large legacy to the Utica Public Library, Trinity College and various other charitable organizations.

Her second son, Lewis Condict was born Nov 25, 1855 and died in an accident on November 29, 1873 as a freshman at Yale College. Third son, Edward Deshon born October 10, 1857 graduated from Harvard College in 1881. He is listed in the City Directories as President of a clothing manufacturing firm and with his brother John became charter members of the Fort Schuyler Club in 1883. He also lived with his mother and is listed in the City Directory until the 1920 edition. A month before his mother died, Edward married Mary Bryant Pratt Sprague (1871-1956) a widow with two daughters and they would have two children, Martina (1906-1959) and John Langdon (1908- 1964). Martina Louise's only daughter, Martina Elmendorf was born October 15, 1861. There is a full account of her life in her own essay also contained in this book.

Even as she dealt with raising her young family, Martina made time to have her husband's sermons published in 1867. In 1872 she joined seven other women from Grace Church in forming the House of the Good Shepherd, a place for poor or neglected children. A small house on Blandina and Kossuth Streets was rented and a matron hired to care for 7 children. The need was so great new facilities at Bleeker and East Street were established to care for 40 children. In 1904, a large brick building at 1700 Genesee Street would provide for 160 children. That facility would eventually move to a new campus in 1959 and continues to care for children today. A Board of Managers of 30 women actually ran the HGS. The officers changed almost every year except for Martina who served as treasurer from 1872 until her death in 1904. Martina also served on the Admissions Committee, the Adoptions Committee and the Finance Committee, in addition to her Board of Managers monthly meetings. How proud she would be to see the HGS is still changing children's lives.

Martina was also among the women from Grace Church to start the Good Shepherd Mission for the people who lived around the old Trinity Church. This mission would become Holy Cross Episcopal Church in 1889 and both mother and daughter would spend much time in supporting this church financially and volunteering in various ministries.

Martina was active in other organizations: Colonial Dames (Martina could trace both parents back to

Martina L. Brandagee became the treasurer of the House of Good Shepherd's in 1873 and served til her death in 1910. This is the second building in 1875.

Colonial times), and the National Association of the Daughters of the Revolution where she was a charter member of the Utica chapter formed in 1893.

After a brief illness Martina died December 10, 1904 at age 78. Her funeral was December 13th in Utica and she was buried in New London, CT. beside her husband. Her long obituary paid tribute to her many community involvements. She left a major legacy in her children and the institutions she started.

Jane Sullivan Spellman

HELEN CURTIS MARSHALL

was born in 1832 in Mohawk, N.Y. the daughter of Alfred (1802-1888) and Susan Peterson (ca.1801-1879) Curtis. She had two brothers Lieut. Lewis Curtis (ca. 1835-1900) and General James E. Curtis (ca.1840-1901).

Helen was educated in Mohawk schools. She was married to Alphonso Delos Marshall (1820-1881) of Mohawk at the home of her parents on September 20, 1877 by Rev. J.G. Lansing of the Mohawk Reformed Church. Helen and Alphonso never had any children. Their home was located on East Main Street in Mohawk, the property extended back to what is today's Marshall Avenue.

Helen travelled worldwide and brought back special plants and flowers to plant in her garden in Mohawk. Her favorite flower to lecture on was the "passion flower". She was even a Class N Judge of flowers and plants at the Herkimer County Agricultural Fair September 14-16, 1880.

Helen was a member of the Mohawk Reformed Church serving as officer of the various societies, which were not listed in her obituary. Helen travelled to Europe with Ex-Senator Warner Miller and his daughter Augusta Miller (Hildreth). Helen did purchase art works during her travels that enhanced her lovely home on East Main Street.

Helen Marshall picture drawing from a faded newspaper by Marge Anderson.

A destitute retired teacher approached Helen for aid, which prompted Helen to organize a group of women from all over the county to interest them in establishing a home for retired teachers. The first meeting was held at her home. Helen, as founder and President, arranged to buy the home of Thomas Cunningham on East Main Street in Mohawk for an Old Ladies Home, which was chartered on October 19, 1895 and incorporated on January 6, 1896. Overseeing the home was a 17 member Board of Managers: Emma S. Morgan, Flora Snell, Ella Stone, Eliza Fox, Minnie Van Allen, Helen Marshall, Ella Churchill, Marcella Usher, Ellen Searles Munger, Elizabeth Gilbert, Helen Case Waite, Addie Rasbach, Amanda Rudd, Ellen Harter, Helen Ingham, Alice Harter and Harriet Russell. Helen was elected as its first President and continued to serve in this capacity until her death in 1910. The Board of Managers was a hands-on group that did all that was needed to keep the building going.

On October 28, 1896 Sallie Howlett became the first resident. The home subsisted mainly on room and board payments, donations, and revenue from various fund-raising events. The founders were smart to recruit a woman from every town in the county to help collect food for residents and to donate items for the constant fund-raising activities. A Board of Trustees was established to look for large donations and bequests. The project became a popular place for donations.

When the "mortgage was burned" in August of 1904, there were 12 rooms. In 1906-07 the east wing was built, making room for 27. In 1962 an addition was built providing 39 rooms.

In 1967 the name changed to the Mohawk Homestead. Another addition was built in 1984. In 1991 it was an ambulatory care home for adults with a fee for service. The 100th anniversary of the home was celebrated in 1995 with room for 42 residents.

Helen's two brothers predeceased her. When she became ill she moved in with her friend, Flora Getman Snell, (Truman) where she died on March 5, 1910. Helen died without a will.

Susan R. Perkins

CHARLOTTE BUELL COMAN

was born in Waterville, N.Y. on November 28, 1833, one of six children of Chauncey and Sarah Winchell Buell. Charlotte's father, Chauncey Buell, was the prosperous owner of a tannery and the Buell Boot Factory in Waterville, N.Y. Beginning in the 1820s his company found a ready market for

boots and shoes in the west where logging and prairie farming required sturdy footwear. As a young girl Charlotte showed talent in art, and when she was only twelve created a detailed drawing of Waterville's First Presbyterian Church. Her parents encouraged her interest in art and even arranged a reception and exhibition of her work. The community came and ad-

Charlotte Coman, a portrait by Ellen Kendall Baker who was born in Fairfield in 1839.

mired her work but the general sentiment was that Charlotte would never be a 'real artist' since at the time many thought only men could become serious artists. She attended Cortland Academy in Homer, N.Y. but had no formal art training in her early years.

In 1857 Charlotte married Elijah P. Coman, son of Stephen and Dorothy Coman of Eaton and the newlyweds moved to Iowa City. With Charlotte's father as a partner, Elijah opened a store selling shoes, boots, and clothing. In a few years the store was doing well and the partnership was dissolved. As the sole owner of a thriving store Elijah was named a director of the First Bank of Iowa. They led a happy life until 1863 when Elijah was drafted for service in the Civil War. He died in combat on October 3, 1864 and Charlotte returned to the family home in Waterville.

At the age of 31, she was a widow with a hearing loss that was growing more severe. Charlotte knew she needed to find a way to support herself and turned to her talent in art. 1870 census records show that Charlotte identified herself as an artist but must have soon realized she needed formal training. For a time she was a pupil of New York City landscape artist, James Brevoort, but longed to go to France to learn in the French tradition. Charlotte's hearing loss made it impossible for her to travel alone. She became acquainted with another aspiring artist near her age, a minister's daughter, Ellen Kendall Baker, of Fairfield, N.Y. It's probable that Ellen traveled to Europe with Charlotte in 1873, perhaps as a paid companion, since it is known that they shared a studio in Paris. There they met British landscape artist Harry Thompson while copying paintings at the Luxembourg. The two became Thompson's first pupils and, with him, explored much of Europe, painting the countryside in the open air. Ellen, a portrait artist, and Charlotte became lifelong friends. Charlotte found a market for her landscape paintings selling them privately and at auction; she was on her way to becoming self-sufficient.

Sometime in the mid-1870s Charlotte returned to New York where she remained for several years. Her French landscapes were displayed at the New York National Academy of Design's annual exhibitions each year from 1875 to 1877, and in 1876, Charlotte's first widely acclaimed work A French Village was exhibited at the Philadelphia Centennial Exhibition. In 1881, after several more years in France, she returned to New York where she made her home for the rest of her life. In 1880 the French publication Art Amateur praised her work, "Mrs. Coman stands at the head of the American ladies who have selected landscape painting for the exercise of their artistic talent. Besides oil paintings, Mrs. Coman has produced some of the best charcoal landscapes ever produced in this country."

Her paintings were noted for what some called 'blue distances', deep greens and blues, overshadowed by delicate mists giving her paintings a lyrical atmosphere. She worked from nature with natural light in the French Barbizon method of plein-art painting rather than in a studio. In her later years Charlotte's work was often light-hearted as when she included elements such as her iconic chickens and detailed barnyard scenes.

Doctors of the day blamed her hearing loss on grief over the death of Elijah but it was more likely caused by a progressive disease of the inner ear such as otosclerosis. In the modern world hearing aids and surgery can ease the isolation of such a loss but they were not available during Charlotte's lifetime. She used a horn, communicated in writing, but never lost her cheerful and outgoing nature. She was amusing and considered a brilliant conversationalist, even on paper! Grateful for excellent eyesight that allowed her to pursue her painting, she felt blessed by her talent, noting that, "Writer, artist, musician has art to constantly uplift and inspire." She even joked that her poor hearing was a blessing because she couldn't hear the negative comments of critics!

In 1885 she built a small cottage and studio in the Adirondacks' Keene Valley where she painted and taught aspiring artists who called themselves "Comanchees". She sketched and painted in New York's Dutchess County and in Pennsylvania, on the Atlantic shore and in St. Augustine, Florida where she went for her health. Everywhere she went she met or became reacquainted with artists, including some very well-known ones such as her long-time friends, British landscapist George Inness, Emile Vernier and Robert Minor. Women were rarely landscape painters so she signed her paintings C. B. Coman hoping to be mistaken for a man since men were paid more for their art. Although she was represented by the well-regarded MacBeth Galleries, Charlotte was always her own best agent and critic. She was prolific and painted until near her 90th year, creating some of her best work after the age of 80.

Charlotte Buell Coman died on November 11, 1924 at the age of 91, not only a 'real artist' but a woman of courage and resolve who overcame her handicap while pursuing her passion for art on two continents. She received many awards and honors during her lifetime but none more prized than President Woodrow Wilson's 1913 invitation to the White House for a reception to view her painting *Early Evening,* which he had chosen as a gift for his wife. In 1905 she received the Julia Shaw prize for "outstanding work of an American woman" and became an associate member of the National Academy of Design at the age of 75. One of her greatest pleasures was to see her work on display in museums and exhibitions. Today her paintings hang in the Metropolitan Museum of Art, Washington's National Gallery, and scores of galleries and private collections here and in Europe.

A watercolor by Charlotte B. Coman is on display at Munson-Williams-Proctor's Fountain Elms in Utica, N.Y.

Joyce Fellows Murphy

SAINT MARIANNE COPE

was born Barbara Koob in Heppenheim, in the Grand Duchy of Hesse-Darmstadt on January 23, 1838. Her parents were Peter Koob and Barbara Witzenbacher Koob. They brought the family to the United States in 1839 and settled at 68 Schuyler Street, Utica, N.Y. in 1840.

Barbara attended St. Joseph's Church and School, leaving after eighth grade. She received the sacraments of First Holy Communion and Confirmation at St. John's Church on Bleecker Street in Utica. At a young age, Barbara felt she was called to join the sisterhood, but she was needed at home to help support her family by working at one of the nearby woolen mills.

After her father's death in 1862, when her siblings were old enough to work and contribute to the family's living expenses, Barbara obtained her mother's permission and fulfilled her dream of becoming a pos-

Saint Marianne Cope

tulant in the Sisters of the Third Order of St. Francis at their motherhouse in Syracuse, N.Y. Barbara took her vows in November of 1863, becoming known as Sister Mary Anna.

As Sister Mary Anna, she was instrumental in the establishment of St. Elizabeth's Hospital in 1866, originally on Lafayette Street in Utica, until moving to its present location on Genesee Street. Sister Mary Anna participated in the establishment of St. Joseph's Hospital in Syracuse in 1870. From 1877 to 1883,

Mother Marianne was Superior General of the Sisters of the Third Order of St. Francis in Syracuse, N.Y.

In 1883, Mother Marianne answered a desperate request from Hawaii seeking help for the missions becoming established there. After long negotiations, Mother Marianne and six other sisters made the long, difficult journey to the Hawaiian Islands to work on the island of Oahu with some of the world's most forgotten people—the victims of Hansen's disease, commonly known as leprosy. The conditions in which these people lived were appallingly bad. The sights, the smells, the physical and mental states of these patients were almost unbelievable.

Gradually, with help from the Hawaiian government and particularly the King and Queen of the Hawaiian Islands, the lepers' care was improved through the pleading and demanding of Mother Marianne who genuinely loved these desperate people. In her special way she taught sewing skills to the women and woodworking skills to the men. But mainly Mother Marianne helped the lepers to know they were loved by God.

The sisters were tireless. When some questioned her, Mother Marianne confidently assured them that they would never contract leprosy despite caring for the wounds and the intimate contact this required. And none of the sisters ever did!

In 1888, Mother Marianne went to Molokai to help Father Damien and care for him as he was dying from leprosy. There she stayed for over three decades seeing to all the needs of the leprosy victims and their families.

Mother Marianne died August 9, 1918.

Finally, after all the years of necessary research and the required number of miracles attributed to her intercession, Mother Marianne was declared a saint in the Catholic Church in December of 2011. She was canonized on October 21, 2012.

Mary Anne Luebbert Buteux

KATE ELIZABETH FOX JONES

was born about 1840, and is listed in the Mohawk Valley Herkimers and Allied Families (#4441) as Elizabeth Katherine the oldest of the six daughters of Frederick Jeremiah and Denise Clark Fox. Her father's mother was Dorothea Herkimer, the daughter of Joseph Herkimer and Catherine Elizabeth Schuyler and a niece of General Nicholas Herkimer. Joseph and Nicholas' parents, Johan Jost and Catherine Petrie Herkimer, were two of the 94 people who settled Herkimer County in 1723.

United Methodist Church of Ilion records report that a Kate E. Thompson married Abner Jones a native of Germany on February 4, 1871. There were three children born to Kate and Abner as written in church records. Jessie baptized June 10, 1874 probably died at three according to the evidence supplied by a cemetery marker in the family plot inscribed 1872-1875. They had a son Paul (1879-1934) and a second daughter Jessie whose existence was established through Paul's obituary. She was still alive at the time of brother Paul's death and was married to a Mr. Allen of Buffalo. The Abner Jones Family lived at 10 Armory Street in Ilion and Abner is listed as a toolmaker.

Kate's public life began in 1883 when she helped organize and became the first President of the Chismore Corp Post #1 of the Woman's Relief Corp (WRC), in Ilion N.Y., the first chapter of the WRC in New York State. WRC is the national organization that began in 1883 as an auxiliary of The Grand Army of the Republic (GAR), the organization of men who fought for the north in the Civil War. The GAR had asked the women to organize an auxiliary at their July 26-27, 1883 meeting in Denver, Colorado. Both organizations worked through local chapters to promote Memorial Day and to relieve the suffering of disabled veterans, war widows and orphans. In the north, WRC was the auxiliary of the GAR but in the south there were WRC units, including units of black women who worked on behalf of disabled veterans.

Kate managed to attend local, state and national WRC meetings and in 1888 was elected National Chaplain. Her job was to assist local chapters in their relief work.

In 1893 Kate was elected President of the New York State WRC. A quote from the *Richfield Springs Mercury* said, "the WCR has chosen an energetic lady of much ability and her selection for so important an office is a compliment to Mrs. Jones and the Ilion Corp of which she is a member." One of her goals was to build a home for women who had served in the Civil War as well as for the wives of GAR members. In 1894 New York State Governor Rosco Flower appointed a Board of Managers to start a Home for Dependent Veterans, Wives, Mothers and Army Nurses. Kate was named to this Board and was on the committee to find the site for the new home. (There was a New York State Home for Soldiers and Sailors at Bath but it had no space for women.) The founding Board visited twenty-two sites before selecting a site in Oxford in Chenango County. The first building was opened April 19, 1897 with 22 residents admitted. By 1911 there were five buildings including four cottages and an infirmary and 172 residents. There is still a veteran's facility there today.

After the term as State President, Kate became a counselor for the National WRC and a Patriotic Instructor. Her duty as counselor was to give assistance to local chapters on how to help those who needed the services that WRC or the government provided. Her responsibility as National Patriotic Chairman was getting flags into the nation's schools. This involved giving speeches throughout the country. Her goal in getting American flags in every school in the nation was met by success including in the south. Her tact and enthusiasm carried the project forward throughout the country.

The *Rochester Democrat and Chronicle* had an article on Kate which was entitled "The Silver Tongued Orator of the WRC". The article went on to describe Kate's nominating speech for Mrs. Shepherd who was running against

Mrs. Carver for National President. The article says "Long before she (Kate) had concluded, the friends of the opposition knew their cause was utterly hopeless and Mrs. Carver's chances of success decreased with every word uttered. Mrs. Jones possesses a wonderful magnetism and she carried the entire convention with her - swayed by her will."

She was directly involved with the National WRC seeking to get the Andersonville Prison in southwest Georgia in the hands of the federal government for a federal park. The prison existed for only 14 months beginning in February 1864 and held over 40,000 prisoners with over 12,000 dying before the camp closed in May 1865. There was an article in 1910 congratulating Kate for her successful efforts when ownership of the prison was transferred to the U.S. Government.

Kate ran for National President of the WRC in 1903 at the convention in Denver and 1906 at the convention in Minneapolis but lost both times. Also in 1906 she represented the WRC at a ceremony to dedicate a tablet on the steamer President Lincoln with influencial guests from around the country .

Kate E. Jones, a picture taken from The Women's Relief Corps annual meeting in 1907.

In 1907 at the convention in Saratoga, Kate was elected National President and would serve the next year. Following her term as National President, she continued to speak at the National Conventions in Rochester, N.Y., Toledo Ohio and Los Angeles, Calif. The 1911 meeting in

Rochester took note that the WRC was the largest body of patriotic women in the world. Kate spoke at many Memorial Day services and gave out prizes and flags all over the state.

Kate had other commitments as well. She was the Conference Secretary of the Women's Foreign Mission Convention in 1899 and reported on the work of the Executive Committee which met in Indianapolis. She also was the Editor of the *Ilion Citizen* (weekly newspaper) *Women's Issue* for the benefit of the YWCA. The writers for this publication were all prominent women in the community. She was involved in the United Methodist Church in Ilion and made time to play the organ there.

Her son Paul studied at Cornell University and his parents would see him join the military with the Mohawk Company during the Spanish American War in 1898.

Her obituary reports she died April 2, 1916 at the home of her son in Des Moines, Iowa. The headline from the *Utica Globe* of April 8, 1916 read: "A Patriotic Woman Who Possessed a Winning Personality Has Died". Her body was brought back to Ilion for an elaborate service at the United Methodist Church. Kate is buried in the Ilion Cemetery with her husband Abner and daughter Jessie.

Jane Sullivan Spellman

ELLEN ELIZABETH "LIZZI" LAVENDER

was born around 1840 in Macon, Ga. as a slave. Although she was one of nine, the names of her parents and siblings are not known.

She was sold at age seven at an auction block for $700, the top price at this time. Mother Lavender would write later of her mother; "My mother was a praying woman though black. At the auction block, she bade me goodbye. She told me to grow up and be good and be a lady, never to 'sass' anybody, but to grow up good and kind. Mother said to me if I don't meet you again here, I'll meet you in heaven". Ellen never saw her mother or siblings again.

Her new owner George Hicks took her to Watertown, S.C. where she became a house slave, taught to weave. She was sold again and became a field hand. Her new owner bred her to a large black man with the intent of creating a breed of larger slaves. Her son Amos was born about 1860.

At the height of the Civil War, her owner's family fled leaving orders for the slaves to protect their possessions. Slavery ended in 1865. She eventually found her way north and worked for the Waterman family in Albany, N.Y. It was here she met with the kindness of their daughter Mary who exposed her to a religious awakening. Ellen would do housework by day and missionary work at night. She made trips to Troy, Lansingburg and Sand Lake.

In the 1880 federal census Ellen Lavender is listed as age 31 with husband Nicholas, age 55, and children: Amos age 20, Grace age 13, Mary J. age 4 and Nicholas age 11 months. They were living in North Greenbush, N.Y. It could be assumed she and Nicholas Lavender had been married around 1866.

In 1883 Ellen came to Utica as a member of the "Negro Jubilee Singers", traveling with Arthur Dixon a black revivalist. She would give lectures on a slave's life. This group traveled all over upstate New York. At one of their performances, a Utica businessman and philanthropist, Edward Curran (1835-1894) was in the audience and convinced Ellen to move to Utica.

Her name appeared in the 1893 City Directory as Lizzie, the widow of Nicholas, living at 6 Madison Lane. Her son Amos was listed as a fighter. In the 1899 City Directory Lizzie was listed as an evangelist living at 39 Elizabeth Street. At this time she was referred to as Sister Lavender.

She provided 'street corner' sermons for anyone to attend. There was one report of a 1894 lecture when Lizzie was talking about Frederick Douglas (1818-1895): "I have often thought that if a man who is only half black can become great like that, what may be accomplished by a person who is all black - like me." Her talks were given throughout the city and were related to her days

Mother Lavendar from a newspaper picture.

as a slave, the need to be close to God and the need for the audience to help feed the poor. Many of the poor were not black but color didn't matter to her.

All her acts of charity were done in the name of the Lord. In 1900 she began the New Year's Day Dinners since she felt it was not good to start off the new year hungry. Over the years these dinners might be at her home or at the African M. E. Mission at 90 Hotel Street near the African Methodist Episcopal

Church at 23 Elizabeth Street. Newspaper reports gave menus and numbers and these varied throughout the years, but all who attended were well fed. In 1928, eight hundred people were served at her annual dinner. Many donations of food or money were given to the cause due to Mother Lizzie's dedication to the needy.

She reached out to house others. In the 1910 Census Elizabeth Lavender was listed as the head of the household with Nicholas age 29, Lizzie age 30, Viola age 6 and 12 other people of different ages and last names. The 1920 listing includes Ellen Elizabeth Lavender, age 77, five family members and Howard Burke age 39, a blind man she took under her wing. In the 1925 New York State Census Elizabeth Lavender is listed as age 80 living in a household of 60 people of all ages and a large variety of names.

She suffered the loss of her two sons. Amos who had married and had five daughters died July 27, 1924 and Nicholas who never married and always lived with his mother, died December 6, 1924.

She died September 9, 1928. She is buried in the New Forest Cemetery on Oneida Street in Utica. Her gravestone reads "Ellen Elizabeth, Widow of Nicholas Lavender, Died Sept. 8, 1928. Aged 90 years". The stone is similar to those given to a spouse of a Civil War veteran.

Sixty years after her death, a group of citizens got together to mark her grave. Malio Cardarelli wrote *Utica's Mother Lavender* in 1999 telling her story. The book ends with this tribute:

> *"Elizabeth, Mother Lavender, through courage and steadfastness of conviction to consign herself to the betterment of others, has earned and richly deserves the everlasting gratitude of the community she served so well for so long."*

> *Jane Sullivan Spellman*

ROXALANA TEFFT DRUSE

was born in 1844 in the Town of Marshall, Oneida County, the fourth of five children of Nathan and Maria Tefft. Orphaned when Roxalana was ten, they all had to make their way at an early age. Roxie worked for her keep on her uncle's farm until she finished the eighth grade and, at fourteen, went to work as a hired girl and seamstress in Utica where she lived with friends or relatives. Every September farmers in the Herkimer County town of Warren hired pickers for their hops and when Roxie was eighteen she joined them. It was fun, the work was easy, and they were given free room and board. Part of the fun was going to barn dances, appropriately called 'hops', where they made new friends, sometimes 'special' ones. It may be that Roxie first met William Druse at a hop.

Bill Druse owned a run-down 90-acre farm on Hogsback Hill Road in Warren, a gift from his father, Stewart, who lived in Springfield in Otsego County. Bill and his father didn't get along; some said an "ungovernable temper" was a Druse family trait. Bill wasn't interested in helping run his father's prosperous farm so perhaps Stewart thought he would be more interested in a farm of his own. Soon it became apparent that Bill was truly no farmer although he managed to keep ahead of his bills by borrowing against his land.

Bill and Roxie had probably known each other a few years before they were wed on May 27, 1865 when she was 22 and he was 38. The difference in age wasn't strange to Roxie; after all, her father had been twice the age of her mother. She admired Bill, thought him very clever, an intelligent man, though a 'very odd genius'. He was a voracious reader and an inventor who had carved an innovative waterwheel for which he hoped to procure a patent. For the first five years of his life Bill had been the cherished only child of Stewart and his wife, Dorcas. Then, in quick succession, three little girls were born to them keeping Dorcas very busy but probably causing Bill to feel abandoned by her. To make matters even worse his father now expected him to do chores around the farm, chores he hated. After years of suffering his father's disapproval, Bill must have basked in Roxie's attention and admiration. She said he treated her well, did anything she asked of him and was 'good enough'.

Roxie had lived in other people's homes for most of her life. Now she finally had one of her own, a former cheese house with rough board floors over a shallow crawl space, just three or four rooms with a loft above, heated by two wood stoves. It wasn't a dream home but it was the only one Roxie was destined to have. Their first child, Mary Jane, was born on February 22, 1866; Ellen called Nellie, followed in 1869 and George in 1875. Remembering the love she had received from a mother she still mourned, she showered affection on her own children. Nellie, who died at ten, was sickly from birth and needed a great deal of care. Once again little girls had usurped Bill's place. Was this what altered his behavior? Roxie said he 'seemed to change', was prone to sick headaches, 'he ran the entire place and we all had to submit.'

As the years passed Bill became withdrawn, abandoning his family for days at a time, often without food or money. He was shabby and unshaven with hair grown past his shoulders. Bill sometimes dropped in on neighbors where he read their newspapers and sat down to share their meals. He was certainly eccentric and some saw him as a harmless character, but even more described him as shiftless, careless and indifferent to his family. No one ever said he was kind or gentle. He became more harsh as time passed, and when he was home abused Roxalana physically and verbally. In the beginning she tolerated his shouted profanities but as time passed she leveled curses at him, too. He threatened to split her brains with an axe, to run her through with his pitchfork or to cut her throat with his knife. He struck her in the face with his fist and beat her with a horsewhip. George said he could not think of a single time his father had been kind to his mother. The lives of Roxie and her children became unbearable. As a loving mother she must have felt guilty that she was unable to provide her children with loving parents and a happy home. She and Mary slept in the parlor where, whispering in the night, they may have tried to come up with a plan. Perhaps it was then that they decided to buy a gun. There is no way to know how they planned to use it.

On December 18, 1884 a violent argument between Bill and Roxie over money came to a tragic end when Roxie shot Bill with the gun her daughter Mary had bought just days before. He was only wounded; Roxie told her nephew, 14-year old Frank Gates, to shoot Bill again or she would shoot him, so he did. Bill was dragged from his chair by Mary who had put a rope around his neck. Roxie then struck Bill over the head with an axe just as he had threatened so many times to do to her. He begged her to stop but she continued striking him until she had severed his head from his body. Roxie dismembered his body and with the boys George and Frank supplying firewood, burned it in the house's two stoves. The terrible stench and thick, black smoke attracted the attention of neighbors who notified the authorities. After a coroner's inquest, Roxie, her children and nephew were arrested and taken by sleigh to the Herkimer County Jail.

There, on the third floor of the jail they had warm beds, a rocking chair and a table. Roxie said, "We have never been so comfortable before in our lives as we have been here. We have enough to eat and good food at that, and enough to wear." Roxie was congenial and friendly with no sign of self-pity. Asked why she did it she said "the devil must have been in me." The trial began on September 24, 1885 with Judge Pardon Williams of Watertown presiding. The District Attorney was Abram Steele, Roxalana's attorney H. DeWight Luce of Richfield Springs. Over a period of three days 133 possible jurors were interviewed and twelve men selected, "fair-minded businessmen and farmers", but they were not Roxie's peers, for women were not allowed to serve on a jury.

The first witness was nephew Frank Gates, aged fourteen, son of Roxie's sister, Lucy. Frank had been living and working as a hired hand on the Druse farm in exchange for his room and board. Frank described the murder and said that Roxie had "been like a crazy person". Despite his part in the murder he had been granted immunity in exchange for his testimony. A dozen or more witnesses followed, including ten-year-old George Druse whose mother wept when he described his life on the farm, his father's neglect, the lack of food and the vicious hostility he witnessed between his parents whenever they were together. Roxie did not take the stand. Judge Williams overruled almost every objection Luce made to the prosecution's testimony.

Roxalana was found guilty of first-degree murder and sentenced to be hung on November 25, 1885. Luce appealed for and won several extensions before his final appeal to Governor David B. Hill who said,

Roxalana Druse, a drawing copied by Jim Greiner from Herkimer Democrat and Ilion Citizen.

"The law of the state made by men is simply in harmony with the law of the Almighty" predicting that "a commutation would only result in more husband killers." Hill moved the execution date to February 28, 1887.

Although the recently passed McMillan Bill limited the number of witnesses at an execution in New York State to twenty-eight, crowds of reporters and spectators thronged the streets around the jail which were patrolled by the 31st Separate Military Company of Mohawk. The hanging did not go as planned. A 213 pound weight created at a local foundry was not sufficient to break the neck of one frail woman, so on February 28, 1887, twenty-eight men dressed in black stood in the cold behind the Herkimer County Jail and watched as Roxalana Druse who weighed less than 100 pounds hung for fifteen minutes strangling before their eyes. She died at 12:04. Roxalana was the last person hanged in New York State, the only person ever executed in Herkimer County. In June of 1888 Roxalana's botched hanging caused legislators to pass a law making electrocution the preferred means of execution in New York State.

Mary Druse pleaded guilty to murder and was sentenced to life in prison. She spent ten years in the Onondaga Penitentiary and Auburn Prison before receiving a pardon, dying in 1915. George became a husband and father but adopted a new name. Roxalana lies in an unmarked grave.

Joyce Fellows Murphy

ROSE ELIZABETH CLEVELAND

was born June 13, 1846 in Fayetteville, N.Y. the daughter of the Rev. Richard (1804-1853) and Ann Neal (1806-1882) Cleveland, the youngest of their nine children: Ann (1839 -1909), William (1832 -1906), Mary (1833 -1914), Richard Cecil (1835 -1872), Grover (1837 -1908), Margaret (1838 -1932), Susan Sophia (1846) and Frederick Lewis (1841 -1872). Rev. Cleveland was the minister of the Presbyterian Church of Fayetteville when Rose was born. The family moved to Clinton, N.Y. in 1851 and to Holland Patent, N.Y. in 1853. Sadly Rev. Cleveland died six months later on October 1, 1853, age 49. Rose known as "Libby" was just seven. The church members raised $1,000 to buy a home for Ann Cleveland and the younger children. Son Grover, age 16 went to work in New York City and then to his uncle in Buffalo to help support the family.

Rose attended Holland Patent schools and was then sent to Houghton Academy in Clinton, graduating in 1866. She taught there for several years and was a friend of Marilla Houghton Gallup whose husband Dr. John Gallup headed the Houghton seminary which he named after his wife's family. Rose taught at the Collegiate Institute in Lafayette, Ind. and at a girl's school in Muncy, Pa. before returning home to care for her mother.

Rose founded the JD'Arc Society, a secret society for young women interested in historical and literary studies and community development. The family suffered the lost of two sons Lewis Frederick and Richard Cecil who died in the sinking of the Missouri on October 17, 1872. Rose kept house for her mother and cared for her until her death July 19, 1882. Ann Neal Cleveland knew her son Grover was Mayor of Buffalo, but did not live to see him elected Governor of New York State in 1883 or President of the United States in 1885.

Rose must have been researching and writing while in Holland Patent since her book *George Eliot's Poetry and Other Stories* was published in 1885. It went into 12 editions and earned Rose $25,000 making her a wealthy woman.

When her bachelor brother Grover moved into the White House in 1885, Rose, age 39, became his official hostess and for 15 months did an admirable job. It was not an easy job for her and she once confessed that to relieve the boredom of the receiving lines, she would conjugate Greek verbs. An article in the *Auburn Daily Press* notes

> *"Miss Rose Cleveland held herself bravely and well in Washington and leaves it with the sincere best wishes of all the country. She is not aggressive or did not attempt to revolutionize Washington ways. She did her best modestly and with dignity as mistress of the White House holding still some of the old ways and old convictions which have been with her for a lifetime".*

Rose was happy to prepare for the wedding of Grover when he married Frances Folsom June 2, 1886, making him the first president to marry in the White House. Relieved of her White House duties, Rose was asked to be editor of *Literary Life Magazine* and she completed her first novel, *The Long Run,* which was not a financial success. In October of 1886, Rose was asked to speak at the National Convention of the Women's Christian Temperance Union (WCTU) in Philadelphia and in 1888

Rose Cleveland, photo from internet sources.

published with Frances Willard, President of the WCTU, "You and I: Our Moral, Intellectual and Social Culture" and "How to Win: A Book for Girls".

In 1890 with the money from her writings, Rose was able to enjoy a trip to the Holy Land and spent the winter in St. Augustine, Fla. One news clip reported Rose invested in some orange groves in Florida and earned enough money to take a two year trip abroad 1892-94 visiting Europe, The Orient, and spending extended time in England, Italy and Switzerland. She returned to enjoy the last year of her brother's second term in the White House attending many of the social functions.

Her financial wisdom led her to invest in 4,500 acres on an island off the Maine coast when the area was just beginning to become a tourist spot. One article reported Rose sold part of her original land for $300,000. She built a cottage and spent summers there.

In 1900 Rose moved to the Maine island while keeping her home in Holland Patent; She would lose her brother Rev. William Cleveland in 1906, her brother Grover in 1908 and her sister Anna Neal Hastings in 1909.

In 1910 she published her translation of *The Soliloquies of St. Augustine,* a book of his early life originally written in Latin.

In 1911, Rose went to Lucca, Italy with her friend Evangeline Simpson Whipple (1862-1930). She was involved in caring for orphans and doing war-related work. Rose died at her home there on November 22, 1918 during the flu epidemic. She is buried in the English cemetery in Lucca and her name is also on the gravestone in the Holland Patent Cemetery with her parents.

Jane Sullivan Spellman

ELLEN MOSS SQUIRE
AKA NELLIE THURSTON

was born Ellen Moss in Lansingburg, near Troy, N.Y. on May 13, 1848. She is the descendant of Edwin and Angeline Moss who moved from Canada to Vermont before arriving in New York State. Nellie's siblings were Juliette, Edwin and Angeline.

Ellen's businessman father was reputed to be a second cousin to one of America's great pioneering balloonists, John LaMountain, who was also living in the Troy area at the time.

Apparently it was this distant family connection that at a very tender age led Nellie to ballooning. Together they would make several document- ed ascensions before the Civil War. A young Ellen would also wed LaMoun- tain in 1864, but the marriage lasted only two years. It was LaMountain who suggested that "Miss Moss," as she was known to the public in early balloon promotional flyers, assume the new name of "Nellie Thurston", a tribute to Ira Thurston, an accomplished early aeronaut who lost his life in 1858 in a ballooning accident.

Another aspiring young balloonist who came under LaMountain's tutelage was a Prospect, N.Y., lad named Herman D. Squire (1840-1911). According to Nancy Squire, a great niece of Herman, at the age of 13, Herman made his first balloon ascension with LaMountain.

At the peak of his popularity, Herman was known as "the most daring and successful aeronaut living." According to several sources in 1859, Herman Squire set a World's record by winning a balloon race from St. Louis, MO. to St. Lawrence County, N.Y.; over 1,000 miles in 19 hours.

It was undoubtedly the LaMountain connection that brought Nellie and Herman together eventually as husband and wife. Nellie was quoted as saying she "had been acquainted with Professor Squire from childhood and had marked his undisputed skill in constructing a balloon as well as managing one."

Eventually, Herman would make fewer ascensions. What he did do, and quite brilliantly, was successfully promoting his wife and their business. Herman used his own Prospect printing press for effective advertising posters, flyers and regular newspaper coverage of their activities, which helped to generate constant demand. Herman also traveled widely "speaking before groups of influential citizens from whom he demanded and got $500 a performance," as one local newspaper reported. In the late 1990's, intact copies of Herman's posters were found by Stan Slusarczyk and the property owners of Herman's Academy Street, Prospect home garage and donated to the Smithsonian's Air and Space Museum in Washington, D.C.

When Nellie Thurston became the first American woman to make a solo ascension in a balloon on July 4, 1871 in Poughkeepsie, N.Y., her fame grew rapidly and she came to be in great demand at fairs, carnivals and celebrations. Her performance at an event was a virtual guarantee of success. In Sterling, IL, Nellie received top billing over President Ulysses S. Grant who was just one of the 25,000 attendees at the fair.

It was September, 1879. The telegraph flashed the bad news announcing the "loss" of Nellie Thurston after a balloon ascension from Carthage on September 5th . Later she would write an account of her thrilling adventures widely published under the title of "Nellie's Story Her Night in the Woods."

She described what happened when deep in the heart of the trackless North Wood, her balloon "Lorne" almost came down to earth:

"I allowed the balloon to descend into the trees; which I am told was about twenty miles southeast from Lowville, thirty-five miles from Carthage. The basket caught on a limb about seventy feet high; I let out a portion of the gas leaving still enough in the balloon to keep it above the trees so as to prevent it from tearing, in hopes of sending someone to rescue it when I found my way to civilization. I then threw open the anchor and went down the rope 70 feet; I next endeavored to fasten the anchor, but as the balloon pulled so hard, I was unable to make it secure; I used all my strength cutting both of my hands badly. A guest of wind struck the balloon and with the seeming power of a locomotive hurled me to the ground, the anchor catching in my clothing, tearing through with lightning force; I barely escaped its entering my side and neck. Getting up from the ground, I saw the balloon high in the air. It was then my heart sank within me; my balloon gone, my clothing torn to shreds, my hands badly lacerated and covered with blood, my body bruised and I in a wet, cold uninhabited wilderness; I knew not where."

This indomitable little lady did survive through luck and pluck. It was an adventure that added another thrilling chapter to her illustrious career.

Nellie made many ascensions in the North Country, including Lowville. Her first ascension was from the old fair grounds on what is now Railroad Street. In October of 1882, at the Onondaga Fair, Nellie drew a crowd of over 40,000 people!

By the early 1880's Nellie's long ballooning career was gradually coming to a close. Between them the Squires ascended 249 times, 140 of them by Nellie.

For nearly 20 years Nellie Thurston was the reigning darling and undisputed "daredevil" of a small group of courageous women balloonists. Especially in the early years of her career, Nellie was widely recognized as "the only female aeronaut in America" according to contemporary newspapers and later books.

Nellie was "All-American", but Canada called her the "first Canadian woman balloonist" because of her father's Canadian roots. The French claimed her as "Nellie LaMont, the celebrated lady aeronaut of France", the only woman included in the 1982 *Catalog of Classic American Airposts and Aeronautica 1784 – 1900.*

Ellen Squire a print from Musings of a Simple Country Man

At a time where the vast majority of women were homebound, Nellie was successfully breaking down gender barriers. She was "flying" through the air at breathtaking speeds 30 years before the Wright brothers barely got their heavier than air contraption off the ground in 1903. Truly she earned the titles of her stage names: "Queen of Cloudland" & "Queen of the Air."

Nellie Thurston was Central New York's leading lady in the early years of area ballooning. In time, other local female aeronauts came along including "Miss Mindy Williams" (Arminda Robenia Williams) of Sherburne. In the 1870s she appeared several times at the popular Brookfield/Madison County Fair. Unquestionably, Nellie's biggest rival in later years was the popular "Carlotta, The Lady Aeronaut" (Mary Breed Hawley Myers of Frankfort, NY) whose married name was Mrs. Carl Myers. "Carlotta," made her first ascension at Little Falls on July 4, 1880. (You will also read about Mary Breed Hawley Myers in this book.)

On January 4, 1932, Nellie Thurston Squire died at the home of Mr. Charles Squire, in Prospect, N.Y., after a long Illness. She was 84 years old. Along with her husband Herman, Nellie is buried at the Gravesville Cemetery, Town of Russia, in Herkimer County, NY.

Lori Gabriel Knapp

ELLEN A. SEARLES MUNGER

was born November 8, 1849 in Belleville, Jefferson County, the daughter of William T and Lucinda White Searles. She had three brothers: George, Rev. Edward and James and a sister Ida.

She was a graduate of Cazenovia Seminary, Cazenovia, N.Y. In Bellville on November 1867, at age 20, she married Henry Gillette Munger (1846-1933) of Camden, N.Y. Henry had attended Falley Seminary in Fulton, N.Y., had worked in Cazenovia, Flint, Mich. and Ellisburg, N.Y. before moving with Ellen to Herkimer to purchase the Taylor Bros. Business. His first store was 19 x 70 feet and he would successfully build a three-story block, which became a shopping destination for all the Mohawk Valley and beyond.

Ellen and Henry's first child Mabel Irene was born in 1869, daughter Bertha Ellen in 1870, son Frederick Searles in 1873, daughter Mary Elizabeth in 1876, Frances Lillian in 1877, Alice in 1878 and Bruce in 1890.

Ellen Munger's home on North Main Street in Herkimer

Not only did Henry prosper in his store, but also he became founder and president of the Herkimer National Bank in 1884, founder and President of the First National Bank of Frankfort in 1888 and became President of the Horracks Desk Company in 1901. His commitment to the community was evident, serving on the Library Board, being a member of a committee of five who organized the Herkimer County Historical Society in 1896, the Herkimer Board of Education, heading Pinecrest Sanitorium and serving on the Christ Church Vestry. He and Ellen built a beautiful home on North Main Street in Herkimer where they entertained often. Ellen was an excellent musician playing and singing with marked skill.

The Mungers would lose their youngest child Bruce in 1893. Ellen, busy with her young family and wife of a community leader who had interests outside the community and who traveled a lot, did become a member of the first Herkimer county-wide organization, when she worked with women throughout the entire county to provide a decent home for retired teachers. Women teachers had to be single and many were destitute at the end of their careers with no family to support them. The county-wide organization bought a home in Mohawk in 1895 and with fundraising activities paid off the mortgage in five years. The first resident entered The Old Ladies Home in October 1896. Ellen served actively on the Board starting 1895 and as its President from 1916-1922. The home was renamed the Mohawk Homestead in 1976 and continues to provide living arrangements for 41 residents.

Ellen become a charter member of the General Nicholas Herkimer Chapter of the Daughters of the American Revolution (DAR) organized in Herkimer in 1896 (The National Organization began in 1891). She would serve as Regent of the Chapter for 11 years and as State Vice Regent in 1906-1908. The DAR worked with the new Herkimer County Historical Society to build a monument on General Herkimer's burial site near his home.

The DAR took a leadership role in helping the Village of Herkimer celebrate its centennial in 1907. The Chapter found and paid for the base for the statue of General Nicholas Herkimer done by sculptor Burr Miller which was unveiled in Myers Park on August 6, 1907 as part of the Centennial celebration.

A year later the statue of Francis Spinner, 1802-1890, a Herkimer native, was brought to Herkimer from the basement of the Corcoran Gallery of Art in Washington. Ellen worked with the General Spinner Memorial Association, a group of women in Washington, D.C. who had been hired by Spinner during the Civil War. As Treasurer of the U.S. from 1861 to 1875, Spinner hired women to cut the new paper money used to pay for Civil War expenses. The G.S. Association tried to find a place for the statue in Washington, but politicians argued over where it should go and the battle went on for 14 years. The Herkimer Chapter of the DAR agreed to pay for moving the seven foot six inch statue to Myers Park and paying for the base and inscription which reads: "The fact that I was instrumental in introducing women to employment in the offices of the Government gives me more real satisfaction than all the other deeds of my life". The statue was unveiled in Myers Park June 29, 1909. Ellen Munger was to be the speaker at the dedication ceremony but was ill.

A major project of the area DARs was to mark the route General Herkimer and his 800 member Tryon County Militia took from his home in Danube to Oriskany where the Battle of Oriskany took place August 6, 1777. The 14 granite stones were placed along the 40 mile route and were dedicated in June 1912.

The area DARs also worked to convince New York State to buy Herkimer's Home in 1914 as a State Historic Site. Ellen Munger was appointed by the governor to serve on the ten person state commission overseeing the site.

Ellen is listed as a member of the Society of Mayflower (#2918) tracing back eight generations to John Alden. Descendents began meeting in the area in 1914.

Weddings for her children were held in 1896, 1897, 1906 and 1908. The first of 11 grandchildren began arriving in 1899. The Mungers would lose their 41 year old daughter Alice in 1919. That year the H. G. Munger Department store celebrated the 50th anniversary of its founding in Herkimer. Ellen sent 50 golden roses to Henry to celebrate.

Ellen and Henry traveled to Atlantic City for several weeks in November of 1923 and continued south to Winter Park, Florida. Her husband was with her when she died February 19, 1924. Her long obituary mentioned her various activities including her work with Christ Church in Herkimer. The funeral services were held from her home with two former rectors of Christ Church officiating. Ellen is buried in Oak Hill Cemetery in Herkimer with Henry and children Alice and Bruce.

Her will drawn September 8, 1909 with her husband, son Frederick and daughter Mabel's husband, Robert Steele, as executors, shows a large estate of $48,567.69 with $43,899.68 in stocks and bonds and indicated her success as a businesswoman. She divided her estate among her husband and five living children. Her daughter Mabel survived her by three years and her son Frederick by six years.

Jane Sullivan Spellman

MARY BREED HAWLEY MYERS,
"CARLOTTA, THE LADY AERONAUT"

was born on August 26, 1850, in Hornellsville, Steuben County, N.Y. Mary was a descendant of the Breeds of Breed's Hill, Boston, and of the Hawleys, settlers of Connecticut. Her parents were John Berry Hawley of Hornellsville and Elizabeth A. Breed of Jamestown, Chautauqua County, N.Y. Her siblings were; John Jay Hawley (born November 12, 18410), Clara Keziah Hawley (born December, 1843), Lilla Elizabeth Hawley (born March 3, 1845), Frank Morris Hawley (born September 22,1848), Miles J. Hawley (born 1853), Ida Hawley (born 1855), Carrie M. Hawley (born 1859 in Jamestown, Chautauqua, N.Y.), and Bertha A. Hawley (born 1863 in N.Y.).

In November of 1871, Mary Breed Hawley married the mechanically gifted aeronautics pioneer Carl Charles Edgar Myers (born March 2, 1842 in German Flats, Herkimer County and died 1923, Atlanta, Ga.). Their daughter, Elizabeth "Bessie" Aerial Myers, was born in 1881.

In his early years Carl was employed as carpenter, mechanic, plumber, electrician and chemist, then banker, photographer and printer. After two years of study of a new object, hydrogen gas balloons, Carl devoted his attention to aeronautical engineering. Already Myers had achieved luminary status when he successfully patented a lighter yet stronger fabric that could withstand the constant folding and unfolding of the balloon during repeated uses.

Mary was a splendid lab assistant and shared Carl's passion for aeronautics. Carl also became known as the inventor of new or improved systems for generating gases and as a constructor of airships in addition to hydrogen balloons, including the aerial velocipede, gas kite, sky-cycle and electrical aerial torpedo.

As she watched her husband ascend in his balloons day after day, Mary decided she would like to fly too. Mary adopted the moniker Carlotta, the Lady Aeronaut (Carl was dubbed "the Professor"). On July 4th, 1880, in Little Falls, NY, Carlotta made her first ascent in a balloon named "Aerial", as a crowd of 15,000 gathered to watch. She took as companions four carrier pigeons which she, at about a mile high, released with news to her Mohawk friends of her flight and of her safe arrival upon earth. She reported a most magnificent voyage, the balloon speeding very swiftly but very gently along until fifteen minutes past five o'clock. After a ride of about thirty-five minutes, in which she traveled nearly twenty miles, she safely landed in a large field on the farm of Mr. John Davis in the town of Stratford near

Mary Myers at a balloon ascension from Congers Park in Saratoga in 1881

the village of Devereaux. All along the route she was seen by the people of the country, many of whom shouted to her and waved their handkerchiefs. As she came near the earth the people on the farm rushed to her assistance and she had no difficulty making a safe landing.

By 1889, Carl had purchased the Gates Mansion, in Frankfort, N.Y., and five acres of land. Here at the "Balloon Farm" (so named due to the large number of partially inflated balloons filling the lawn) with its spacious living quarters, was room for their chemical laboratory, a printing press, carpentry and machine shops, a loft for cutting out and storing balloons, gas generating equipment, shipping rooms, and water pumps.

Mary collaborated in many ventures with her husband. Together they conducted experiments, gave ballooning demonstrations in the summer months, and patented a balloon glide-control device that they claimed gave them some control of the balloon's movements. They spent the winter months studying aeronautics, navigation and meteorology. Myers saw nothing unusual in her activities, attributing their success to her knowledge of balloon construction, the steering device, and her good health.

Mary's balloon ascensions became extremely popular at fairs and resorts and were financially very remunerative. In addition to New York State, she flew in Michigan, Ohio, Indiana, Massachusetts, Connecticut and Canada, One of her most popular summer ascensions, starting in 1881 and lasting for the next ten years, was from Congress Spring Park in the resort city of Saratoga, N.Y.

Not all ascensions were smooth sailing, however. In 1882, from Congress Park, Mary's balloon got caught in a cyclone, and she had a truly frightful flight. Her flap-valve cord broke, causing some loss of control, and she landed in a tree. On her ascension on July 2, 1883, from Ottawa Canada, Mary's balloon, known to be in poor shape, ruptured at 10,000 feet. Mary parachuted and safely landed in the trees.

In 1883, Carl published a pamphlet entitled: "Aerial Adventures of Carlotta or Sky-Larking in Cloudland, Being Hap-Hazard Accounts of the Perils and Pleasures of Aerial Navigation" written by Carlotta. She wrote about the adventures leading up to their invention of a "screw-sail and rudder-kite" steering apparatus which she first called "Sky-Lark" and, later, "Flying Dutchman."

In 1886, from Franklin, Pa., Carlotta tested her husband's idea of using natural gas instead of hydrogen. Due to a sticky valve, she reached an altitude of 21,000 feet (approximately four miles high), a world record. As notable as the record itself is the fact that she ascended to this height without oxygen equipment, yet she suffered no ill effects.

The synergistic Myers couple also toured France, Spain, Germany and Russia from October 1888 through July 1889, exhibiting their aeronautic skills, taking balloon orders and, to paraphrase the Wizard of Oz, hobnobbing with their fellow aeronautic wizards.

Daughter Bessie joined her mother on an epic flight in 1888, from Syracuse. Their balloon was lacking ballast due to excess passenger weight and ended in a terminal velocity descent into a lake. Bessie saved the day by crawling along a half submerged log, towing the balloon and her mother ashore. Bessie never made another free-flight.

Bessie did, however, "dazzle the crowds at the World's Fair" in St. Louis, Mo., in 1904, by pedaling her father's inflated, cigar-shaped "Sky Cycle" through the air of a large auditorium without ever brushing against the walls or roof.

After a career of superlative performances, managing the Balloon Farm, and bringing up her daughter, Carlotta retired from public performances in 1891. She continued as a test pilot until 1910.

In 1908, as a result of a challenge made by the owner of Campbell Airship Company of Brooklyn, N.Y., Mary flew a pedal-powered airship named "Zephyr" from the Washington Park baseball grounds in Brooklyn, across the Brooklyn Bridge to New York City Hall, across the Hudson River to Jersey City Hall, and landed in Secaucus, N.J., in one hour. She was promised and presented with the "handsomest gold badge ever given to an aeronaut."

Two inspiring children's books relate Mary's exploits, *The Balloon Race* (I Can Read Book #3) by Harper-Collins, and the Canadian publication, *The Lady Aeronaut* by Joanne Stanbridge. A permanent NASA Science Museum exhibit acknowledges the Myers' contributions to promoting safer, more scientific aeronautics. Arcadia's Images of America Series, "Frankfort, N.Y.," features their beautiful, still-standing Victorian mansion (the "Balloon Farm") on the cover.

In 1910, daughter Bessie, who became Mrs. Newton C. Wing on June 12, 1912, moved her parents to her home in Atlanta, Ga. after they sold the Balloon Farm. Bessie and Newton's son Roger was born in 1914. Mary passed away in Georgia in 1932, at the age of 83.

A state historic marker was unveiled at the Balloon Farm in November 1998 as part of the Commemoration of the 150th Anniversary of the Women's Rights Convention in Seneca Falls, N.Y.

Lori Gabriel Knapp

HARRIET E. RUSSELL

was born on February 13, 1851 in Falls Church, Virginia. She was the oldest child of Albert Newton Russell (1826-1913) and Mary Hatch Russell (1830-1905). Her siblings included two brothers: Samuel T. (1853-1929) and George R. (1861-1932) and a sister, Ella M. (1855-1944). It was in 1861 that A. N. Russell relocated his wife and children to the Mohawk Valley settling in Ilion where he began working for the Remington and Sons Company as Superintendent of Freight and Transportation. Several years later, he opened his own company. A.N. Russell and Sons was a prosperous lumber and woodworking business which expanded several times over the years to accommodate new products.

The Russell family had an impact on the history of Herkimer County during the latter half of the 19th century and the beginning of the 20th century through business endeavors as well as their civic-minded activism and generosity. Camp Russell in Woodgate was given to the Boys Scouts by Samuel in 1918. Then in 1923 he donated Russell Park in Ilion to the village in his father's name.

The family resided at 100 Otsego Street, the present day site of Whiter-Hendrix Funeral Home. In 1913 after their father's death, Harriet and her sister Ella moved to 61 Second Street directly across the street from the Ilion Free Public Library which Harriet played a prominent role in developing. Both brothers married. Samuel and his wife had four children, and George, who married twice, had three children.

Harriet and her sister Ella were among a group of six women who had the distinction of being the first graduating class of Ilion High School in 1873. Her course of study enabled her to become a teacher and later principal of the intermediate department in Ilion. She left teaching in 1890 to travel and pursue other interests. As the daughter of a prominent businessman she did not have to work to earn a livelihood.

Harriet soon embarked on a five-month journey to California with her father. She described her 10,106 mile trip in a journal full of vivid descriptions of people and places. Later that year, she and 32 other women formed The Travelers Club whose purpose was to offer members opportunities to increase their knowledge as well as develop powers of thought and expression. Twice a month members researched topics to be presented to the group. Two examples of the topics presented by Harriet were: "Epoch Making Rulers" and "Native Americans, Indians and Alaskans". She served as the President of this group from 1908 to 1910.

In 1891 Harriet stood before a meeting of the Ilion Alumni Association as she explained the need for a public library. A small library that had been housed in the school had been previously destroyed by fire. The alumni, convinced of the importance of a public library in Ilion, took up a challenge given them by C. W. Seamans, a wealthy businessman. Mr. Seamans was a partner

No likeness of Harriet Russell has been found. This is the interior of Ilion Free Public Library 1893.

in the firm of Wyckoff, Seamans & Benedict which purchased the typewriter business from Remington. Seamans promised to build the library on land donated by him if the group could raise $5,000 in a year. The alumni's fundraising activities were successful and even surpassed the goal. Plans for the library pushed forward. It is interesting to note that Harriet's father, A.N. Russell, was entrusted by Seamans to do the actual building of the library and served as Superintendent of the Construction Works.

The beautiful Ilion Free Public Library built in Romanesque style opened on Friday, October 27, 1893. The Village Board appointed Harriet E. Russell as the first president of the Library Board. The Ilion Free Library became a model of what a small town could accomplish and how a library could be successfully operated. The *Utica Morning Herald* reported in 1899 that the library had 9,300 volumes and 2,379 readers. "For a town of 4,500 the circulation is remarkable. The number of books withdrawn for home readership in a year was 43,315." The library became a focal point of the community with people taking out books and community groups holding meetings there. The library continues today to provide materials and services to patrons of all ages for their personal enrichment, enjoyment and educational needs.

In 1895 Harriet joined the drive to find suitable housing for retired teachers who had little or no money on which to live out their later years. She became part of the original group of women who started "The Old Ladies Home". Its first resident was accepted in 1896. Harriet served as treasurer of the county-wide Boards of Trustees overseeing the home for 32 years. This facility whose name was changed in 1967 to The Mohawk Homestead is still caring for adult residents in a home-like environment following a vision formulated by a group of compassionate women.

Harriet was a member of the DAR and Shakespeare Club. She was a devoted member of the Methodist Episcopal Church and the Missionary Society.

In 1929 the headlines of the *Ilion Sentinel* read: "Harriet E. Russell Leaves the Library Board". After 37 years of continuous service ill health compelled Harriet to give up her position as President of the Board of Trustees of the Ilion Free Public Library. The board was reluctant to accept her resignation citing her many years of dedicated leadership.

Following her death in December 19, 1935, she was buried in the family plot in Armory Hill Cemetery in Ilion. In her will she generously donated money to the Old Ladies Home and the Methodist Episcopal Church. What she also left behind was her imprint on creating solutions, building on ideas and maintaining levels of quality to make life better in her time as well as for the future.

Barbara Sabo Dunadee

DELIGHT EVANGELINE RANSOM KELLER

was born in1853 in the town of Manheim, Herkimer County, N.Y., the daughter of David E. (1805-1890) and Rebecca Ann Aldrich (1819-1922) Ransom. She had three brothers: Albert (1846-1853), Charles W. (1849-?) and Bryon A. (1851-1896) and six sisters: Hannah (1837-1931), Mary E. (1840-1892), Lucy A. (1842-1853), Lefa Ann (1855-1943), Lillian B. (1853-1893) and Effie May (1861-1861).

Delight was educated at the Little Falls Academy. She attended Cazenovia Seminary, Cazenovia, N.Y. in 1871.

Delight married Willard Keller (1850-1937) a widower, on October 13, 1875. They had two sons: Charles Byron (1876-?) and Albert Monroe (1881-1971) and five daughters: Harriet (1885-1916), Laura Adella (1879-1946), and Orpha Edith (1878-1934).

Delight was a charter member of the Rock City Chapter of Order of the Eastern Star, an organization that began nationally in the 1880s for female relatives of Master Masons to share the benefits of knowledge and self-improvement Freemasonry makes to men.

Her participation in the National Organization of the Daughters of the American Revolution (DAR) organized nationally in 1891 was extensive. In 1906 Delight served as Regent of the Astenrogen Chapter of the DAR in Little Falls, a chapter organized in 1895. On June 9, 1909, Delight was the organizing Regent of the Colonel William Feeter Chapter DAR in Dolgeville. She was both a National and State Chairman of the DAR for a number of years and on the National Committee for the Preservation of Historic Spots.

In 1898 when Delight was with the Astenrogen Chapter, she joined with the Oneida County and Herkimer County Historical Societies in getting the monument erected over the grave of General Nicholas Herkimer. Delight originated the idea of marking the 40 mile route General Herkimer and the Tryon County Militia took August 1777 from the General's home

Delight Keller photo taken c. 1910

to the Oriskany Battle Site. With the help of area DAR Chapters, 14 large boulders with attached plaques were dedicated on June 14, 1912 and are still in place today. Most importantly, Delight secured a state appropriation for the purchase and preservation of the General Nicholas Herkimer Home. This enlarged brick house, built in 1764 was in terrible shape when the state of New York purchased the building and grounds in 1914. Today this New York State Historic Site has been beautifully restored and opened for visitors who want to step back into history.

She was also a member of the Little Falls Grange and the Pomona Grange of Herkimer County, organized nationally as Patrons of Husbandry in 1870s, an organization for farmers, both men and women. It provided social and cultural events for farm families.

Delight served as President of the Herkimer County Women's Christian Temperance Union which began nationally in 1874. This organization dealt with the abuse of alcohol that many thought was destroying families.

She was a member of the Lutheran Church known as the "Old Yellow Church" in the town of Manheim. Delight was active in the Woman's Home and Foreign Missionary Society of the Lutheran Synodical Society of the State of New York.

Delight died on Flag Day, June 14, 1933, age 80. The funeral was held at the Little Falls Presbyterian Church. She was buried in the Yellow Church Cemetery on Yellow Church Road, in the Town of Manheim, Herkimer County, N.Y.

Susan R. Perkins

LUCY CARLILE WATSON

was born in Utica on February 10, 1855 to William H. Watson, M.D. and Sara T. Carlile Watson. Her brother William Livingston was born in 1856. She was educated in Utica at the Young Ladies Seminary and at the Utica Academy. Her Academy graduation essay was titled "The Pressures of Society upon Belief." Lucy's family members were community leaders, and her father served as Surgeon General of the State of New York, and he served on the New York State University Board of Regents. Watson Place in Utica was named for him.

Lucy Watson spent her adult life working for community improvement, with almost two decades dedicated to women's suffrage. Susan B. Anthony spoke in Utica in 1894, but five years elapsed before an organization dedicated to suffrage formed officially. Lucy Carlile Watson was among the charter members who in 1899 organized the Utica Political Equality Club. In 1900 Lucy was elected president and she served in that capacity until 1917. In 1900 the local suffrage movement was inspired when Rev.

Lucy Carlile Watson

Dr. Anne Howard Shaw, physician, Methodist minister and national leader visited. Momentum for suffrage grew slowly in Utica and the surrounding region, but Lucy Watson and her dedicated associates persevered. In 1912 the New York State Suffrage Convention was held in Utica. When interviewed by the *Utica Herald Dispatch* on August 31, 1912, Lucy said: "women suffrage appealed to my sense of justice…. Equal suffrage for men and women is an essential feature in a democracy." After the 1913 defeat, across the state tenacious suffrage groups unified and developed new strategy. Lucy Watson led the campaign in central New York, and in 1914 she was thrilled to see public support mounting. That year Carrie Chapman Catt was a dynamic visiting speaker and Lucy Carlile Watson, as grand marshal of the suffrage parade, was the visible regional leader of the movement. Her photograph and statements were featured in a long article in the *Utica Daily Press* on June 14, 1914.

The following year in July, suffragists staged a statewide demonstration, which began at Montauk Point and ended in Buffalo. On July 15, 1915, Lucy Watson carried the suffrage torch from Utica to Buffalo. *The New York Times* on October 31, 1915 acknowledged Lucy Watson's leadership in this description: "a gentle, sweet-looking woman, whose hair is beginning to turn gray, is the generalissimo of the very aggressive host of suffragists here." That year Lucy promoted regional efforts in the counties of Oneida, Herkimer, Fulton, Hamilton and Lewis. She told the Times interviewer: "We have made a good fight, and if all the men who have promised to support us keep their word we shall win…we feel very much encouraged over our reports from the rural sections of the district." Women's suffrage was victorious in New York State in 1917, a few weeks following an event on October 17, 1917 at the Avon Theatre in Utica where Carrie Chapman Catt and William Jennings Bryan were featured speakers.

Its work accomplished after nineteen years, the Political Equality Club disbanded on December 27, 1918. Lucy Carlile Watson's contributions were appreciated and she received recognition for her many years of dedicated and effective local and state leadership when she was selected by the League of Women Voters to be among the 100 New York women listed on a bronze Suffrage Memorial Tablet in the Capitol in Albany. Lucy Watson later campaigned for women to serve as jurors.

When the New Century Club incorporated in Utica on December 13, 1893 to promote social, literary and artistic endeavors, Lucy Carlile Watson participated as a charter member. She served as recording secretary in 1896, and as vice-president in 1897, the year the large brick auditorium designed by Frederick Gouge was constructed on the east side of the 1826 brick headquarters on the corner of Genesee and Hopper Streets. During Lucy's presidency1899-1903, the New Century Club published the *Outline History of Utica and Vicinity,* which continues to be a valuable resource on Utica history, noteworthy citizens and natural surroundings.

Lucy Watson was co-founder and vice-president of the Central Association for the Blind. She endowed a room and served as president of Utica Memorial Hospital Board of Trustees. She served on the Board of Managers of the House of the Good Shepherd and was active in the Utica Playground Association. In 1912, Lucy Watson helped found the Child Welfare Committee of the Municipal League of Utica. Later, this group, which worked with nurses and doctors to improve the infant death rate, was called the Baby Welfare Committee. Eventually the Visiting Nurse Association assumed those responsibilities. The State Charities Aid Association and its efforts to assist tubercular children were of special interest to Lucy Watson.

Lucy was active at Grace Episcopal Church in Utica, and she served on the planning board of the National Cathedral in Washington, D.C. She was a charter member of Oneida Chapter of the DAR and was active in Colonial Dames and Descendants of the Mayflower.

Prior to her death, the Business and Professional Women's Club of Utica honored Lucy Watson "in recognition of her work for women in the community, state and nation." Following her death December 12, 1938, Utica Mayor Vincent Corrou said: "The death of Lucy Carlile Watson removes from Utica one of its outstanding citizens. Her activity in civic, religious and charitable circles will always place her definitely in the memories of all Uticans." She is buried in Forest Hill Cemetery, Utica.

Lucy Watson was predeceased by her brother William Livingston Watson (1856 to 1908). Her survivors included Alice Watson Doolittle, Watson Lowery, Lucy Carlile Lowery, Lois Andrew Doolittle and Alice Parkinson Doolittle.

Virginia Baird Kelly

ELLA MCKEAN EDSALL

was born in Prattsville, Greene County, N.Y., in 1857, to Albert and Louisa McKean. When her parents passed away, she was adopted by Harvey and Lila Sikes. Ella was 10 years old at this time. She was educated at the Prattsville Academy and the Misses Greens' Finishing School for Girls in New York City. She also studied at the New York College of Music.

Ella married Dr. Irving S. Edsall in 1885. Irving Edsall, was born in 1858, a son of William and Jane Swartout Edsall of Delaware County. Following his graduation from Albany Normal School, he taught school for a time before entering Albany Medical College, graduating in 1885. The young couple moved to Middleville in Herkimer County where the doctor began his medical practice. They built a home on Herkimer Street (Route 28). Middleville was an industrial village containing a tannery and knitting mill. Smaller local businesses also provided employment. The Herkimer, Newport, and Poland Narrow Gauge Railway passed through Middleville where trains were repaired and painted. Farmers from miles around came to Middleville to deliver their milk for shipping to the downstate markets and to shop for their daily needs. Life was exciting in the busy village.

In 1890, a son was born to Ella and Dr. Edsall. They named him William Sikes Edsall (1890-1916). Later they adopted a daughter named Sigrid Rantanen, from a local family. Always a prolific reader, Ella continued to read while caring for her family.

As Ella neared the age of forty her household duties lessened affording her more time for community involvement. Her love of reading and her position in the community caused her to consider combining these ideas in a study club. Dr. Edsall was a supportive husband and joined her in the formation of the Middleville Literary Union in 1898. One of the first study groups of its kind in New York State, it soon became very popular. Meetings were held every two weeks in local homes. Members prepared papers for presentation to the group ranging from the classics and current events to history, Shakespeare, poetry, and travel. Membership lists show that most of the area clergy and their wives joined the M.L.U. as well as school principals, teachers, businessmen, housewives, and farmers. It is remarkable that so many residents of a small community participated in a study group that involved so much preparation on the part of members. The M.L.U. continued for almost a half century. The last recorded meeting was in 1946.

Ella's next idea received the support of community residents of all ages. She decided that a public library was necessary and called a meeting to create local support. The year was 1914 and a great many citizens turned out for the event, including several young men. Enough donations were received to start the library and by December 1914, officers were elected, with Ella serving as president. A Provisional Charter was granted to the Middleville Free Library in 1915. Ella obtained Polish books for the many

Ella Edsall photo which hangs at the Middleville Free Public Library

Polish immigrants arriving in Middleville to work in the industries. The library continued to serve Middleville residents under the leadership of Ella Edsall. She became known as the "mother" of the library. In 2015, the Middleville Free Library celebrated its Centennial. From a small collection of books in a tiny room located in a tiny building to spacious quarters in Middleville's Corey

Hall with an extensive collection of books and other media and an array of computers, the library continues to serve the public.

Two years after the founding of the Middleville Free Library, young William Sikes Edsall was killed in an auto accident a few miles from the Edsall home. William had graduated with a degree in mining engineering from Northwestern University, but returned to Middleville to live because of his father's poor health. The loss of their only son was a frightful blow to the Edsalls, but they continued their good work in the community. Their daughter, Sigrid Rantanen, became a school teacher in nearby Herkimer.

Following the death of Dr. Edsall in 1924, Ella moved to Herkimer where she participated in community activities with her usual zest. She taught a class in the Methodist Church, belonged to the DAR, and was active in the Eastern Star. Following a stroke, Ella died in her home on Park Avenue, Herkimer at the age of 83. Filed among her papers was a letter she had written in 1938, giving directions for her funeral and information for her obituary. She was buried in Prattsville beside Dr. Irving S. Edsall and William Sikes Edsall.

Jane Winterbottom Dieffenbacher

CORINNE ROOSEVELT ROBINSON

was born September 27, 1861, the youngest of four children of Theodore Roosevelt Sr. and Martha "Mittie" Bulloch. Her father was the fifth son of merchant banker Cornelius Van Schaack Roosevelt and Margaret Barnhill of the Oyster Bay Roosevelts of New York, and her mother was a self-confident and headstrong Georgia belle. They married at her family plantation north of Atlanta in 1853 and came north to New York City to live.

*Corinne Robinson 1890 picture from
The Roosevelt Women*

As children, the four young Roosevelts, all born within eight years, tended to be sickly, and Corinne suffered from asthma and allergies. Believing strenuous physical activity to be beneficial, her father installed an outdoor "exercise room" at their 20th Street brownstone. With her siblings and various cousins and friends, Corinne was tutored at home by her aunt Anna Bulloch, who had come from Georgia in 1857 to live with the family. Grandmother Bulloch had also joined the household, and the atmosphere during the Civil War years was occasionally tense as sympathies of North and South were debated. After the war, when she was seven, Corinne visited Georgia with her parents, but so much was changed that any southern ties soon faded.

Corinne's education extended far beyond any formal lessons in her home classroom to include natural history walks and visits to museums. Discussions at the family dinner table might be held in French and frequently centered on topics to stimulate the children's curiosity and interest in current affairs. From an early age Corinne was encouraged to speak up and hold her own with her older brothers and sister, and she would come to thrive on public speaking to audiences of any age. Summers were spent with the extended family at Oyster Bay, full of physical activity and literary adventure. Her closest friend during these years was Edith Carow, who would later become her brother Theodore's second wife.

College was never a consideration for young ladies of Corinne's social standing, but extended tours of Europe were considered a required part of a proper education. On her first trip abroad in 1869, when she was eight, the family spent a year traveling through England, Holland, France, and Italy, often with private tutors. Back at home, she continued to demonstrate her energetic and adventuresome spirit when she was the first to ride an unbroken pony her father brought home for the children. She would always exemplify a family motto, "Over or under, but never around."

In 1872 a second trip abroad took place while the Roosevelt's newhouse on 57th Street was being built. This time, the family visited Egypt and spent three months on a houseboat on the Nile river, tutored by older sister Anna ("Bamie"). The three younger children went on to board in Dresden while they studied German. There, Corinne wrote her first poem, "The Lament of an American Child in a German Family." In 1878, life as she knew it ended when her father, Theodore, died at the young age of 45.

By 1880, Corinne's brother Theodore had graduated from Harvard and married Alice Lee of Boston, and Corinne had made her debut into New York society at an elegant affair at the family home. Her days were spent reading, riding, walking, discussing books and ideas, and maintaining a full social schedule. Soon she was introduced to Douglas Robinson through her brother Elliott (later the aimless and erratic father of Eleanor.) Six years older than she, he had been born in Scotland of American and Scottish parents and was a graduate of Oxford University. He was making a fortune in real estate in New York but was considered a plain person with a bland personality. For him it was love at first sight, and the Roosevelts encouraged the match. But Corinne, wary, reluctant, and fearful of losing her independence, put off the wedding for two years. Finally, on April 29, 1882 they were married at the 5th Avenue Presbyterian Church.

Their first child, Theodore Douglas Robinson, was born the following April. He would later marry Helen Rebecca Roosevelt, a sixth cousin and niece of Franklin, and become a New York State Senator and an Assistant Secretary of the Navy. Within six years three more children joined the family: a daughter Corinne ("Corinney") in 1886, Monroe in 1887, and Stewart, Corinne's favorite, in March, 1889. Six months later she and Douglas joined family members on a trip to the Dakota Badlands where she impressed ranchers as an accomplished horsewoman.

On February 14, 1884, a double tragedy had occurred in the family. Corinne's mother, Mittie, died of typhoid fever, and brother Theodore's wife, Alice, died following childbirth. Two years later Theodore married Edith Carow, Corinne's childhood friend. Corinne's life as wife, mother, and socialite continued as before, managing three households and moving among them. These included the 61st Street mansion in New York City, a seventy-two acre estate in Orange, N.J., and the Robinson family's summer home, the Henderson House, in upstate Herkimer County. About this time she hired Josephine Poirot from France to be her personal assistant, and traveling companion.

In 1894 the Robinsons rented out their New York City house and made the Orange estate their permanent residence. The rural lifestyle was good for the children, and it was an easy commute to Manhattan for Douglas. Corinne supervised lessons for the children, taught Sunday school, continued to travel, and developed close friendships with both men and women who shared her literary and artistic interests.

In 1900 Corinne and Douglas attended the Republican convention when brother Theodore was nominated for vice-president. When he became president the next year following the assassination of William McKinley, Corinne became a frequent visitor to the White House. For the next seven years she spent weeks at a time in Washington enjoying the winter social season and immersing herself in the political atmosphere. She was always supportive of her brother, whom she sometimes referred to as "The Big Stick," and kept herself abreast of presidential affairs. When Theodore received unabating criticism for inviting Booker T. Washington to dine at the White House, Corinne indicated her support by entertaining him at her New York mansion. During a six-month trip to England in 1902 to enroll Corinney and Monroe in school she was treated like a celebrity as "the President's sister".

After the death of Douglas's mother Fanny in 1906, plans were made by the family to memorialize their parents by building a new library for the village of Jordanville near Henderson House in Herkimer County. On August 26, 1908 the Robinsons, with guest President Theodore Roosevelt, dedicated the new neo-classical building before a crowd of hundreds and then entertained invited guests at a reception at Henderson House. Corinne and Douglas would always be revered for their gift to this rural community.

The following February a tragedy occurred that would devastate Corinne for years to come. Her son Stewart, a student at Harvard University, fell from his dorm window and died instantly. She was shattered by the death of her favorite child and suffered immensely from this loss. Later that year, after her daughter Corinney was quietly married to Joseph Alsop, Corinne, Douglas, and son Monroe left for a trip around the world. While visiting Italy, Egypt, India, China, Japan, and Korea, she found solace in new surroundings and in writing poetry. At the same time her health concerns worsened, especially arthritis and failing vision, which would trouble her for the rest of her life. Eventually she would lose the sight in one eye and endure as many as sixteen surgeries to preserve what sight remained, some aboard ship while traveling.

When she returned home she resumed her public life: speaking, writing, charitable activities, and politics, limiting herself to four evenings out per week. She maintained a close relationship with her brother Theodore; later, his decision to run as a Bull Moose Party candidate was made at her home in Manhattan. Her circle of close friends included author Edith Wharton, Senator Henry Cabot Lodge, and Charles Allen Munn, editor of *Scientific American.* In 1911 Scribners published her first volume of poetry, *The Call of Brotherhood,* followed by *One Woman to Another* in 1914, and *Service and Sacrifice* in 1916. Her public speaking career expanded, especially in presidential politics, as she appeared for candidates at meetings and rallies, her schedule managed by a speakers' bureau. She also spoke on favorite authors, women in politics, problems of divorce, love of country, civic duty, world travel, and her brother, Theodore. Occasionally she could be heard on the radio. In 1916 she was active in the attempt to defeat Woodrow Wilson for reelection and in helping her son Theodore win his bid for the New York State Senate.

In 1918 Douglas died suddenly in Amsterdam, N.Y. after suffering a heart attack on the train from New York to Henderson House, sons Theodore and Monroe were in the Army, and Corinne moved into a smaller house on East 63rd Street. Her brother Theodore died in 1919, and she wrote a biography, *My Brother Theodore Roosevelt,* which was serialized in Scribner's Magazine. She gave a spirited address at Bloomfield's Hotel in Richfield Springs on the Women's Memorial Roosevelt Association and spoke about her brother's love of country at a reunion of the 121st Regiment in Jordanville.

The Republican convention of 1920 provided Corinne with a history-making opportunity when she became the first woman to give a major address at a nominating convention of either major political party. Before 14,000 delegates at the Coliseum in Chicago she seconded the nomination of General Leonard Wood for President. Later she was singled out as the outstanding orator of the day and applauded for her ability; she easily emerged as the most popular of the prominent Roosevelt women. She was named, with six other women, to the Executive Committee of the Republican Committee, and continued an expanded schedule of public speaking, thriving on her travels to major cities around the country.

In 1921 Henderson House remained closed for the summer as Corinne toured post-war Europe, visiting battlefields and lecturing on the life of her brother. Her fourth volume of poetry, *The Poems of Corinne Roosevelt Robinson,* was published in 1924, and in 1928 she campaigned for Herbert Hoover, appearing at a debate on his behalf at the courthouse in Cooperstown. That year her vote for governor went to her fifth cousin, Democrat Franklin Roosevelt. A fifth book of poetry, *Out of Nymph,* appeared in 1930, and her last surviving sibling, sister Bamie, died.

In 1932 Franklin was nominated for president, but Corinne could not openly work against him in favor of Hoover, neither could she actively support Franklin. Her vote, however, went to FDR.

On January 17, 1933 Corinne was suffering from a respiratory infection, but she insisted on attending a party at the Waldorf Astoria for First Lady-elect Eleanor, her favorite brother's favorite child. Her condition worsened, and she died in her Manhattan home on February 17 at age 71. She was buried in the family cemetery at Henderson House.

Donna Loomis Rubin

EUGENIE STEVENS

was born in Rome, New York on Thursday, August 8, 1861, to Edward Livingston Stevens and Frances (More) Stevens. Eugenia graduated from Rome Free Academy and later attended Mrs. Piatt's Female Seminary in Utica from 1879 to1880.

Eugenie's mother, Frances More Stevens, was born October 12, 1835, in Roxbury, New York. She died June 19, 1875, and is buried in the Rome Cemetery. Eugenie's father, Edward Livingston Stevens, was born March 10, 1834, the son of Stoddard Stevens and Annadine Beardsley. He was a prominent member of the bar and was elected the last President of Rome in 1869, as Rome was incorporated the following year, but later served as mayor of Rome from 1877 to 1878.

Eugenie had one younger brother, Stoddard More Stevens, born in 1863. Like Eugenie, he attended Rome Free Academy. Following his graduation from Cornell University in 1885, he practiced law. His wife, Katharine E. May, was the daughter of George A. May and Harriet Bacon.

Eugenie's father was married again in 1876 to Clara Catlin of Ripon, Wisconsin, giving Eugenia three half-brothers; Edward Livingston Stevens, Jr., born 1877, Harrold B. Stevens, born 1879, and John Hoyt Stevens, born 1885. Eugenia's father died November 10, 1900, and is buried in the family lot in the Rome Cemetery.

Eugenie Stevens and her brother, Stoddard, were both active members and served as officers in the John More Association through their mother, Frances More. The John More Association, Inc. is an association of descendants of one couple, John and Betty Taylor More, who immigrated to the United States from Rothiemurchus, Scotland, in 1772 and were among the first European settlers of Delaware County, N.Y. This association is currently active and holds reunions annually.

A charter member of the Wednesday Morning Club in 1892, Eugenie served as one of its early secretaries and was active in the organization for the rest of her life. When the Mohawk Valley Library Club was created in 1903, Eugenie was appointed treasurer. She was a member of the Woman's Club starting in 1915, served as president from 1930 to 1931 and corresponding secretary from 1931 to 1932. She served as treasurer from 1932 to 1934 and again from 1935 to 1938. She also chaired its Community Service Department for some time. In 1917, Eugenie became a life member of the local chapter of the American Red Cross. She was a member of Fort Stanwix Chapter, Daughters of the American Revolution, serving as Regent from 1922 to 1925. At the Zion Episcopal Church, Eugenie taught Sunday School and was affiliated with its Parish Aid Society. In spite of her dedication to numerous service organizations, Eugenie also found time to act as chairman of the Women's Club Saturday afternoon bridge parties and was very competitive in tournament bridge.

Eugenie Stevens directed the Jervis Public Library from a postcard in 1906.

In March of 1895, Eugenie was appointed Assistant Librarian by the Board of Trustees of Rome's Jervis Library. Eugenie worked under Marjorie Elizabeth

Beach, the first librarian, a former teacher and a grandniece of John B. Jervis, after whom the library was named. In February of 1901, Marjorie Beach requested a six-month leave of absence due to poor health and the board of trustees arranged to have Eugenie do Miss Beach's work during her absence for $15 a month starting on March 1st. As it turned out, Miss Beach did not return to the library and resigned her position in September of 1901. Eugenia was appointed Head Librarian.

It was in the second year of Eugenie's appointment as Head Librarian that the first telephone was installed at the Jervis library, allowing her to accept reference questions by telephone. She fielded a variety of questions in all disciplines with the reference books at hand, but was herself well-versed in popular culture and was able to provide impromptu shelf talks on authors from Arthur Conan Doyle to Zane Grey.

Miss Stevens advocated opening the library on Sundays. She had been attending the state library conferences where statements regarding Sunday opening had been circulated. "The most important part of the State's citizenship is deprived of proper access to the library, if no provisions are made for Sunday opening. A man confined to his labour every day but Sunday should be able on that day to take his share of the public benefit provided by the State."

Many other libraries including those in the city of Utica and the village of Herkimer opened their reading rooms from 2:00 to 6:00 on Sundays, although they did not allow books to be checked out. Checking out books came too close to violating the Sunday Laws (commonly known as Blue Laws) which prohibited the sale of many items on Sunday, including books. While it may have been the only day that a working man might have access to the library, it was also the only day for him to go to church and to spend time with his family. The board allowed the library to open on Sundays but, due to lack of popular demand, the experiment was discontinued after a short time.

Eugenie Stevens served as Head librarian at Jervis Library until 1921. But she did not lose interest in the library with her retirement. She later served on their Board of Trustees in various capacities. For most of those years she had been chairman of the board's important library committee, which is in charge of books and staff. She was elected President of the Board in 1928 and was still serving on the board as Vice-President at the time of her death.

Eugenie Stevens died on August 8, 1940 her 79th birthday. She is buried in the family lot at the Rome Cemetery.

Roberta Seaton Walsh

MARTINA ELMENDORF BRANDEGEE

was born October 18, 1861 to Rev. John Brandegee (1823-1864) and Martina Louise Conduit Brandegee (1825-1904), whose essay is also in this book. Martina was only three years old when her father died. With three older brothers, John E. (1853-1906), Lewis (1851- 1873) and Edward D. (1857-1933), it was not surprising she was a tomboy. She attended local schools and graduated from Utica Free Academy in 1880. The family home was at 515 Kent Street in Utica and she lived there until her death. When she was 12 her brother Lewis, a freshman at Yale University, died and she would travel to New London, Conn. to bury her brother next to her father.

While she attended daily services at Grace Church, Martina along with her mother, became very involved with the Good Shepherd Mission that became Holy Cross Church. She played the organ for 45 years at Sunday services at Holy Cross as well as accompanying the music with her lovely contralto voice.

From 1896 until 1937 Martina E. had choir activities at Holy Cross Church which influenced the entire area. Her choir began with 13 boys and over the years 290 men and boys were involved. The yearly choir dinners and picnics she organized and paid for were events for the whole community. As the neighborhood around Trinity Church was settled by Italian families, she insisted the services be said in Italian. There was also a playground near the church and she would get involved with baseball games. She also covered the cost of any windows that were broken. Her charity to the families was great and she invested in the young people's careers at every opportunity. She continued to use a horse and carriage (horse and sleigh in winter) for her trips around town to deliver food or assist local families until her death.

One of the examples of Martina E.'s determination to have things done correctly (i.e., her way) occurred when the Bishop came to dedicate at Holy

Cross Church, a cross that was to be put on top of the steeple. Martina insisted that she and the Bishop be hoisted to the top of the steeple for the dedication instead of remaining on the ground while only the cross was hoisted.

Martina would lose her mother on December 11, 1904 and her bachelor brother John the following May. Her only remaining bother Edward was abroad at the time and

Martina E. Brandegee from a picture in 1952 article by Gloria Santucci.

she was responsible for having the funerals in Utica and their burials in New London. Brother Edward had married Mary Bryant Pratt Sprague, a widow with two children in November of 1904, and he would maintain home and businesses in Utica, residing with his sister until 1920 and living with his wife in Brookline, Mass.

Martina E. did take a trip to Europe in 1926, but she had all her responsibilities covered while she was gone. Her constant involvement with both Grace and Holy Cross Churches and the people in each church was total and many benefited from her generosity.

Her last brother Edward died in 1933, a few hours after giving his daughter Martina, away at her marriage to James Lawrence, Jr.

Martina's will attests to her excellent business sense since her list of investments was long with very successful stocks. She seemed to have survived the 1929 crash. When she died July 9, 1937 at age 76, she left an estate of $351,866.31 which went to Grace Church, St. Luke's Hospital, the Diocese of Central New York in trust for Holy Cross Church and to her brother Edward's children, Martina Lawrence and John L.Brandegee.

As with all her family, the funeral was held at Grace Church but she is buried in Cedar Grove Cemetery in New London with her parents.

Martina Louisa Brandegee and Martina Elmendorf Brandegee, a mother/daughter combination, contributed in many ways to help others in their community from 1854 to 1937, an 83 year span.

Jane Sullivan Spellman

KATE LOUISE LOFTUS WELCH

was born September 9, 1862 a few miles north of Clinton, N.Y. the daughter of Thomas Loftus and Ann McDermott Loftus. Her parents moved to Forge Hollow a few months later. Kate and her siblings (James, Mary, Patrick and Rosalie) grew up on the family farm there.

Kate's early education was in a one-room schoolhouse. She dedicated her life to learning and service. Her self-education came from books as well as the people and natural world around her. She taught in various Town of Marshall one-room districts: Hanover, Brothertown and Forge Hollow. Her services as tax collector gave her a knowledge of all the people in her Town of Marshall.

Kate Loftus lived in this house by the side of the road.

Kate became engaged to Martin Welch (1861-1917) but broke their engagement when Martin got drunk one evening. In later years she regretted her decision and did marry him on May 13, 1891. They lived happily in what they called "The House by the Side of the Road". Kate described him in one of her columns: "He was a man of quiet nature, kindly, helpful to others, a good neighbor and a thoroughly good citizen. Mr. Welch ran a farm at Forge Hollow, and he did it successfully. He was an industrious man, honest, and upright in all his dealings, and was held in the utmost respect by all who knew him."

Kate was an avid reader of famous poets and was very fond of James Whitcomb Riley. Lord Tennyson and the Scottish poet, Robert Burns, were other favorites. The works of George Eliot (aka Mary Ann Evans 1810-1880) caught her imagination.

In 1898 Kate began her column "Along Willona Creek" for the weekly *Waterville Times*. She filled her column with tales of people, animals, flower and fauna. Her prose was full of joy and wonderment of all that was around her. In this column Welch told the stories of her valleys, the birds, the deer, the woodland, plants, the trees, and the caves which she described in poetic words. Here is an excerpt from one of her columns:

> *"Sometimes richly dressed men, women and children descended from the heavy coach into the sylvan shade and looked with approval on the romantic beauty of the rock-and-pond bordered gorge, in those days musical with the celestial voices of wood and hermit thrushes and countless veeries which homed on the wooded cliffs. There were scarlet tanagers too, flashing through the dense foliage, dipping their flaming coats in the foaming waterfall or on the blue surface of the pond."*

Her life became the center of her writing, both prose and poetry. Her books of poems *Idylls of Willona Creek* was published in 1919 and a second volume *Hearts and Flowers* was printed in 1929.

She was a gardening enthusiast who wrote gardening advice, spoke to garden clubs and acted as a judge in flower shows. She was interested in opera and other types of music, art, literature and astronomy.

In a 1947 newspaper article entitled "Along the Oriskany", David Beetle said: "Kate Welch seems to have gotten the name of the Creek from the 'West Branch of the Oriskany' (an original name) and 'Big Creek' (that's what the unemotional 1907 surveyor called it) to 'Willona'- not a bad accomplishment even for a poet if she had done nothing else. But Mrs. Welch, tall, angular, effusive, friendly, taught a lot of Forge Hollow youngsters as well."

This tribute appeared in the *Waterville Times* after she died April 23, 1934.

> *"In the death of Mrs. Kate Loftus Welch not only her relatives sustain a loss but every reader of the paper. Her contributions have attracted much attention and have been read with pleasure and profit. She found so much in life that is good and passed it along to others. Truly she was a noble woman, a kindly soul, and a lady who by her every deed gave an example to emulate. From nature she found many an inspiration which only a cultivated mind could find."*

She was survived by her two sisters Mary Russell (Mrs. Dennis B.), Utica and Rosalie Hamilton (Mrs. Homer), Norwich and brother Patrick Loftus, Utica. Her funeral was conducted from the William J. Walsh Funeral Home in Clinton followed by a Requiem High Mass from St. Bernard's Church in Waterville. Kate is buried beside Martin in St. Bernard's Cemetery.

Richard L. Williams

HARRIET BLACKSTONE

was born November 13, 1864 in New Hartford, N.Y., the daughter of Mills Case Blackstone and Elizabeth Ladd Blackstone. Edward, three years older than she, was her only sibling. She attended the Home School for Girls where she studied music, drawing and language, the traditional courses of study for women of her day. After graduation she taught children drama and drawing.

When the Blackstone family moved out west to Illinois in 1883, facilities for art study were limited and Harriet instead became a teacher of

A likeness of Harriet Blackstone.

drama, art and elocution at Gales High School. In 1901 she published a book of speeches called *New Pieces That Will Take Prizes,* a guide for students in public speaking contests. Harriet was 38 years old when she gave up teaching elocution in Galesburg.

As her interest in becoming an artist herself increased, Harriet moved to Brooklyn and began formal study at Pratt Institute under William M. Chase who greatly influenced her use of color. To pay for her tuition and board, she continued to teach drawing classes. Harriet was an adherent to academic tradition; she saw herself carrying on the traditions of old masters.

A Mrs. William J. Underwood, wife of the general manager of the Milwaukee Railroad, recognized Harriet's talents and became her friend and patron. Mrs. Underwood accompanied Harriet on her first trip to Europe in 1906. Harriet then took an apartment in Paris to study classical art and technical drawing methods with Jean Paul Laurens at the Julien Academy. She viewed the paintings at the Louvre and focused especially on Leonardo da Vinci, choosing him as her mentor. She referred to him as "Papa" and would sometimes try to draw with her left hand as he did. Her interpretation of Leonardo in a mystical sense was done in 1925 and is called The Prophet.

Her painting, Soldat de Crimee, of an elderly veteran of the Crimean War, was accomplished and accepted for exhibition in the Paris Salon in 1907. It was given permanently to the National Gallery of Art at the Smithsonian Institution. Harriet jubilantly returned home to her one-story bungalow on the north shore of Lake Michigan in the hamlet of Glencoe, Illinois, where she and her mother lived together. Harriet began a full length portrait of her mother just after they moved into the new house. The elder Blackstone was getting ready to go to church and stands serenely. This work was included in Harriet's first public exhibition.

The Blackstone bungalow was built in 1905 at a cost of $3,500 in a quiet woody setting that was yet within easy walking distance to the railroad station and electric cars. By 1910 Harriet had earned enough from her portrait commissions to add a studio to the property known as "Brushwood". Wide casement windows from floor to ceiling afforded plenty of natural light for her to work. Generally she felt a sense of restfulness at her studio, surrounded by antiques and traditional furnishings. Most of her things had been in the family for four generations. Harriet kept a large collection of books, some first editions.

A colonial style fireplace of brick extended to the ceiling. Friends, musicians and writers would gather around the open hearth and hospitable fire on Sunday afternoons when she entertained at congenial teas and displayed her artwork. "She has made an individual abilding place," said House Beautiful magazine.

In the summer of 1913, Harriet returned to the continent and enrolled in Chase's six week painting class in Bruges, Belguim. She toured Italy, Gibraltar and Spain. Well inspired by what she had seen – the famous artists, Harriet began to feel more dissatisfied with her portrait artistry. She felt she had not realized her full potential and wrestled with her soul to produce the paintings she felt. "To become a great artist, one must be a great and noble soul, with courage to hang on, truly of marvelous energy, endowed with genius, sometimes bordering on insanity," she believed.

In 1918 she was appointed by the government to paint artillery targets at Taos, New Mexico and took advantage of the opportunity while there to paint a Pueblo Indian girl.

In 1920 Harriet sold her property in Illinois, settled her mother with her brother Edward on his farm in Maryland and moved to New York City. Eventually her studio was located in the famous old Chelsea Hotel where half a dozen artists had studios and were to become famous. Harriet "set up her easel with all its good luck charms – the horseshoe magnet, the lucky stars and a picture of a rabbit in a red coat."

Two years later she exhibited a stunning portrait of Mme. Galli-Curci, the operatic star of *La Traviata*. The singer appears enveloped in ephemeral atmosphere, – rare, delicate and opalescent in color. Miss Blackstone preferred about eighteen sittings at three day intervals for a finished portrait. Her work in that field was now flourishing. Harriet was elected to the National Arts Club, 15 Gramercy Park, Manhattan which awarded her its Club Prize in 1934. Harriet was a member of the International Society of Arts & Letters and the League of American Artists.

An interesting story is told of how the painting of pianist Stell Anderson came about. Harriet often covered a canvas with many tones and washes of paint before leaving it to stand, waiting for the proper sitter or inspiration. Stell and her friend Esther Morgan McCullough happened to attend an exhibit at the Dudensing Gallery where she was fascinated by what she saw and spent the entire afternoon studying Harriet's paintings. In turn, Harriet was struck by the pianist's great presence and spiritual nature. She showed her the previously painted canvas thickly painted with greens, golds, oranges, russets and burnished browns. The canvas was the ideal backdrop for a proposed full length portrait of Anderson and was received very well. The coloring kept with Anderson's personality and reflected her high spiritual qualities. "The eyes of the pianist have an expression of infinite sweetness as though the spirit enjoyed an inspired existence." Harriet spent two months in Vermont completing the Anderson commission and doing other portraits – one of which was the widow of the governor of Vermont. It was 1936 and Harriet was 72 years old.

Thirty of the thirty-five paintings exhibited in the 1984 Bennington, Vermont show called A Mystic Vision, were in Miss Stell Anderson's private collection. Miss Anderson's care preserved the paintings of her friend, Harriet Blackstone. A biography that another friend, Esther Morgan McCullough, wrote went unpublished.

Portraiture is the highest branch of painting, demanding knowledge of humanity and uncovering particular qualities to show the charm, strength and individual characteristics of the sitter. Harriet did not 'pose' her subjects but rather watched and studied them, absorbing their personality. When she painted children, she would let them play and romp around the studio, capturing their movements with her brush. Charles Underwood at eleven years of age, Huse Dunham, Rosemary Ames and Harriet Leonard are some of the favorite children portraits. Simplicity was the key. A most successful group picture was of six children of the Thorne family, standing, reading and seated at the table in their library. The painting speaks to the fact that American children are as charming as the French children seen frequently on exhibit.

Harriet's outstanding canvases included portraits of Madam Plevitzkaia, Alfred McDonald Compton, Alma Thompson Matteson, Anna Morgan, Mrs. William A. Talcott and Rebecca Lowrie. She painted Judge Truesdale surrounded by his two grandchildren.

Miss Blackstone was represented in the Butler Institute of American Art in Youngstown, Ohio, Vincennes Art Association, the M.H. de Young Memorial Museum in San Francisco and the Layton Art Gallery in Milwaukee, Wisconsin. Harriet's work was displayed in the Brooklyn Museum and the National Portrait Gallery in Washington, D.C. and the National Museum of American Art at the Smithsonian. She also exhibited at Carnegie Institute. In March 1941, a memorial exhibition of Miss Harriet Blackstone's works was held at 460 Park Avenue Gallery in New York City. Eighteen painting were on view to show her "full range as she progressed from society portrait painter to artist of mystical vision".

In 2011 an exhibit in Peoria, Illinois showed lesser known Illinois women artists. Harriet Blackstone, one of these sixty-three women, held a place in this exhibit called "Skirting Convention: Illinois Women Artists, 1840-1940." Critics said her canvases were distinguished and had quality. Harriet rose to become one of the most prominent portrait artists of her time.

Harriet died in New York City of pneumonia on March 16, 1939. She was 75 years old. A service was held at the Little Church Around the Corner in Manhattan. Her burial took place in New Hartford at the East Hill Cemetery where she joined her parents. Her obituary appeared in various papers throughout the state, but was only three short paragraphs long.

Miss Blackstone's papers are in the collection of the Archives of American Art. This cryptic note was found tacked to Harriet's easel when her friends emptied her New York studio after her death: "Why is Art the only lasting expression of that life beyond life that man has sought through the ages?

Janice Trimbey Reilly

LORETTA O. DOUGLAS

was born July 8, 1865 in Saxonville, Massachusetts, the daughter of Andrew and Adelia Bremen Douglas. Both parents were immigrants: her father coming from Scotland at the close of the Civil War, her mother a native of County Meath in Ireland. She had two brothers: Dr. Fred J. Douglas (1869-1949), a surgeon in Utica and congressman from the 33rd district, and Dr. Edgar H. Douglas (1867-1910), a physician and mayor of Little Falls.

It was in 1871 that the Douglas family moved to Little Falls, N.Y., when Andrew Douglas became the Superintendent of Gilbert Knitting Mills. Educational performance in school was held in high esteem by Mr. and Mrs. Douglas. All three children, after graduating from Little Falls Academy, went on to college: her brothers to Dartmouth and medical study, Loretta to Cortland to take a four-year classical course majoring in languages. She also studied public speaking at Syracuse University, attended summer school at Cornell and obtained her master's degree from Wesleyan University in Bloomingdale, Ill.

She began her teaching career in Cazenovia, followed by five years in Stamford in Delaware County. In 1892, she started teaching Latin and Greek at Ilion High School on Morgan Street in Ilion. A promotion to head the school's English Department followed four years later. In 1906, she was appointed principal of Ilion High School. In 1914, a new high school was opened on Weber Avenue as Principal Douglas continued her leadership role. Her tenure as principal lasted fourteen years until 1920. A source of pride for Loretta as principal was that the high school maintained a regents record second only to one other school in the state, and Ilion ranked fourth in the state for the thoroughness with which it prepared students for college.

On June 28, 1917, at the Silver Jubilee of the Ilion Alumni Association, members from 25 graduating classes presented Principal Douglas with a purse of gold in gratitude for her years of dedication to the students. Frances T. Giblin, class of 1878, handed out the award, saying: "We have here one who has played an important part in the world's history through scholars trained. Who for a quarter century has aided in developing the child and in aiding the success of the man and woman. One who has spent many anxious hours seeking to find the best methods to develop the varying qualities of the individual."

Loretta Douglas in photo from 1920 Ilion High School End of Year Booklet.

An ingrained devotion to duty and a high sense of honor drove her to instill on young minds virtues of moral value. As principal, she stressed that her students should do good and shun evil. She expected much from her graduates as future leaders. At an Ilion Alumni Banquet in 1935, Loretta, as the guest speaker, spoke of "citizenship, intelligent cooperation, patriotism and upholding righteousness as rights and likewise duties." Her feelings concerning her graduates were quite apparent as she continued in her speech to say: "The abiding joy of my life is my alumni. I would like to see the boys and girls of Ilion High become real power for good in the village, the state and the nation."

After leaving Ilion, she accepted a position at Utica Free Academy teaching English. She remained there for ten years, retiring in 1930. She was 65 years of age.

During her years in Ilion and Utica, Miss Douglas kept an outstanding record of accomplishment, as she never had a student fail. She was well respected by the Regents Education Department in Albany having spent several summers working there. Harry DeGroat, a former principal of Cortland Normal School and supervisor of New York State Regent Examiners, called Loretta "One of the greatest of all teachers Cortland Normal School has produced in its history."

Loretta enjoyed traveling, having gone on trips to Scotland, England, Switzerland, France, Italy and Canada. She was a well-known public speaker with a talent to entertain and enlighten audiences. The stories and speeches she told to her audiences were rich with vivid details. Her varied repertoire included telling captivating Christmas stories, travelogues, and oratories on history and literature. Three examples of the topics she entertained audiences with were: "The Life of Harriet Beecher Stowe", "Outstanding Contributions by Women Since 1840 in Literature" and "Ten Rivers in Literature."

She was a member of the Grace Episcopal Church of Utica and Secretary of its women's auxiliary. She was also a member of the Travelers' Club and the Shakespeare Club of Ilion, the Republican Club of Utica, the New Century Club, the Western Group of College Women, the YWCA and the Utica Hobby Club.

In 1944, at age 78, she was interviewed for an article in the series "People Worth Knowing" for the *Utica Observer-Dispatch*. Loretta said this about her chosen career path: "Girls then hadn't much choice among professions. Teaching was about the only 'lady-like' ambition a girl could entertain." Loretta also stated that she would go right back to teaching then with the same zest she felt for the profession a half century before.

Also in 1944, the Ilion Alumni Class of 1917 started a scholarship in her honor. This gesture indicated that 27 years after leaving the school, her former students still held her in high regard.

Always interested in hearing about her alumni, Loretta attended every Ilion Alumni Banquet until 1945, when illness prevented her. On her eightieth birthday in July of that year, several of her former students visited her and presented her with 80 roses. She died four months later on October 18, 1945 at St. Elizabeth's Hospital in Utica. Pallbearers at her funeral were all former students. She was laid to rest in the family plot in Little Falls.

Loretta was an influential educator and principal, who spent 46 years shaping countless lives. She is fondly remembered for her dedication to her students.

Barbara Sabo Dunadee

ELLEN HARRIET CLAPSADDLE

was born January 8, 1865 in South Columbia, Herkimer County, the only child of Dean and Harriet Beckwith Clappsaddle. Harriet Beckwith's grandfather served in the War of 1812 and became a member of New York State's legislature, both in the Assembly and Senate. He was a staunch abolitionist.

The Clapsaddles (Klebsatel), a Palantine German family, were among the first immigrant settlers in the Mohawk Valley, arriving from Wurtemburg in 1733. The Clapsaddle clan owned the flats, about 100 acres, lying east of Otsego Street and extending from Main Street south to the foothills in Ilion, N.Y. in Herkimer County.

In 1777, Augustus, aka Denus Clapsaddle was commissioned as a major in the Tryon County Militia, 4th Regiment, known as Col. Peter Bellinger's. He served with General Herkimer and was fatally wounded in the Battle of Oriskany (his name is on the monument there); his wife and children were left to survive as best they could. Their log cabin was destroyed later in an Indian raid. The Clapsaddle sons and grandsons worked the rich fertile land and improved the farm through the years that followed. When the Erie Canal was dug through the front portion of the property, its value increased. In 1828, John Clapsaddle sold the property to Eliphalet Remington for $2,800 to "build his works," the Remington factory that manufactured Remington firearms. Later, the Remington Typewriter factory would also be constructed.

One of Major Clapsaddle's sons was Denus. He and his wife Elizabeth Frank had twelve children, the oldest was Lawrence. Lawrence's son Dean (Ellen's father) was born in Columbia, N.Y. in 1803. He was a blacksmith in Richfield Springs from 1828-1835, and continued the business in Mohawk until 1858. Dean was also a postmaster at Columbia. He later became a farmer.

Ellen showed artistic ability before she could read or write. She was educated in a small one-room schoolhouse on the corner of Prey Hill Road and McKoon Road in South Columbia until the 8th grade. From there she attended Richfield Springs Seminary, an academy equivalent to high school education today; it prepared young ladies for higher education or college. She graduated in 1882.

Ellen Clapsaddle as a young woman, the source is unknown.

She studied at Cooper Union Institute for the Advancement of Science and Art in New York City; there, a student could work to pay for their tuition. Ellen was not from a wealthy family. When she left Cooper Union in 1884, she returned to Richfield Springs where she gave painting lessons in her home for the next fourteen years. China, she herself decorated, was in demand locally. Ellen had also been hired by Mr. Ibbotson, a coal dealer at the time, to design the company's brochures and booklets in their printing shop on Church Street in Richfield Springs.

In March 1898, the Richfield Springs newspaper reported that "Miss Ellen Clapsaddle is considering the question of a two-year trip abroad with attendance and expenses paid for herself and mother. The offer comes from the International Art Publishing Company in whose employ she is, in the capacity of artist and designer." With the death of her father in 1891, Ellen became particularly close to her mother, and the two traveled together. They eventually returned to Richfield Springs where Ellen free-lanced, doing landscapes and portraits, especially of folk who lived in Richfield Springs. There is only one known portrait that has survived - that of a boy carrying a crutch; its whereabouts is unknown.

Working later in Europe, her talents became refined, more detailed. Her children's images blossomed; Clapsaddle postcards were distinctive. Her designs were of smiling children on St. Valentine's Day, St. Patrick's Day, Thanksgiving Day and other holiday scenes. Patriotic cards depicted George Washington, but not Abraham Lincoln for some reason. Her Halloween postcards have become the rarest of all.

Ellen turned the mean looking Kris Kringle into a jolly loving Santa Claus. In July 2012, the Moore Postcard Museum offered a reproduced series of four Christmas cards, featuring a little girl who starts out going to bed, praying, sleeping and waking in the morning to find toys, but never actually seeing Santa who appears in the background. The original postcards were sent in 1908 and 1909. Each postcard was printed with a little verse illustrative of the drawing; the verses were written by Ellen.

In 1890, Ellen drew her first "snow baby." Dressed in fluffy winter white coat and leggings, a girl held poinsettias, evergreen trees or holly. Three cherubs slid downhill on a red sled. The script read: "May happiness and all that makes thy Pathway bright, be with you." Snow baby look-alikes in miniature statues grace the shelves of many gift stores today.

Artists have found it difficult to duplicate Ellen's children's faces, to correctly proportion them. The styles of her children's clothing are historically recorded through Clapsaddle's works. The daintiness and originality of each piece made her works remarkable. Booklets, watercolor prints, calendars, trade cards and other objects in the world of advertising appeared, but her postcard and greeting card business was the most successful.

Ellen was a slight, pretty woman; and even though she gave the impression of being shy, she showed a determination to prove her worth in the artistic field and set off alone for life in the big city shortly after her mother's death in 1905. Her connection with New York City had begun in 1898, when the International Printing Company paid for her artistic services.

Some references say that Ellen established the Wolf Company, which was backed by the Wolf brothers, and was a subsidiary of the International Art Publishing Company of New York City. Some other sources suggest she was employed by the Wolf brothers. However, it is clear, Ellen was one of the first female souvenir/postcard artists of the era to be established. She was the sole artist and designer of the company – this alone was a great contribution to society.

Ellen and the Wolf brothers invested heavily in Germany's engraving and publishing firms. Germany was known for excellent printing with four colors, printing on quality paper with quality inks. Ellen worked closely with a German engraver, overseeing her designs, checking the colors. She traveled to Germany often. Ellen was on her way to becoming a millionairess; she and the Wolf brothers prospered financially and they reinvested in the German firms.

When World War I broke out, association and communication between Germany and America ceased. The German plant where Ellen's artwork was stored was fire-bombed; her work was lost. She was nowhere to be found. Ellen had witnessed the war first hand; her spirit to live gone. Wandering the streets, hungry, sick and penniless, Ellen was then 55 years old. Her mental capacities were broken.

By 1917, the golden age of postcards was over. The Wolf brothers borrowed money so they could search for her in Europe. Their company had gone out of business. They found her and brought her back to the United States. Ellen was admitted to the Peabody Home in January 1932, where she spent the next two years until her death from chronic nephritis.

Ellen died January 7, 1934 – one day short of her 69th birthday at the Peabody Home, Pelham Parkway in New York City. Her remains were eventually transferred from the potter's field site in the city, to the gravesite of her parents through the generosity of friends and admirers. There is a simple marker in Lakewood Cemetery in Richfield Springs.

One cousin, Mamie Chase of Richfield Springs, was mentioned in her obituary as her only survivor. Jim Parker who presently lives on Clapsaddle Farm on Rte. 51 in Ilion is a distant cousin. Mr. Parker is a folk artist and conducts a year-round farmer's market on his historic property where he sells note cards and reproductions of Ellen's paintings. He often entertains groups with his presentations of Ellen Clapsaddle's work. Evelyn Edwards of Clinton, N.Y. has been a collector of her postcards for many years and also has presented programs. Ellen's greeting cards, both old and newly reproduced, can be found on-line.

Ellen Clapsaddle was one of the most talented, and prolific American postcard illustrators. Her drawings are just as appealing today as they were one hundred years ago.

Janice Trimbey Reilly

JESSIE MOON HOLTON

was born in 1866, in Ilion, the eldest daughter of Clinton A. (1827-1992) and Frances (Hawkins) Moon (1831-1890). Several months later, her parents moved to the Town of Russia where her two siblings were born; Anna Florence in 1870, and Howard in 1874, who died a month later. The family lived on a farm in Town of Russia before moving to Newport, N.Y.

Her father was educated at the Fairfield Seminary in Herkimer County, N.Y. He entered Union College in Schenectady, N.Y. as a junior, in 1853 where he was Phi Beta Kappa. He studied law with J.H Wooster in Newport, and was admitted to the New York State Bar in 1857. He taught at Fairfield Academy for two years, and became the first county school commissioner for the 1st Assembly District when the New York State Board of Regents initiated a new structure for all schools. He lived in Herkimer for several

Jessie Moon Holton, age 18, assistant teacher at Herkimer High School in 1894.

years where he served as a District Attorney in 1861-62 before joining the 121st Regular Company C to fight in the Civil War. Due to a wound he was forced to resign in 1863; he then moved to Ilion as a partner of Thomas Richardson, attorney for the E. Remington and Sons Company. He moved his family to the Town of Russia near his father's farm and "mingled legal business with farming" until the family's move to Newport in 1876, resulting in his full-time law practice there. His progressive views of women's suffrage and education supported his daughter's entrance to Cornell College in Ithaca N.Y. Respect for women and education provide the foundation for Jessie's life story

By age eighteen, Jessie was an assistant teacher in the local union school district where her father served on the district's original school board. Her dedication to education advanced quickly; Jessie held positions locally as assistant to the principal, and then as a teacher at Fort Plain's Liberal Institute, where Carolyn Hough Arms, her eventual colleague, was a student. Jessie's mom died in 1890 and her father in 1892, coinciding with life decisions that would take Jessie far from Herkimer County.

At the age of 24, Jessie married Frederick Holton and moved with him to Washington, D.C., when, as a young attorney, Frederick went to work in the U.S. Patent Office. Frederick was supportive of his wife's desire to continue her career, and she accepted a teaching position at Mrs. Flint's School, a small and fashionable institution in its time. Jessie encouraged her friend, Carolyn Arms, to become an English teacher at the same school. They taught together for several years until deciding to open a school of their own. Their entrepreneurial spirit was forced to quickly gain traction, as they were immediately dismissed from Mrs. Flint's employ when she learned of their plans. Fortunately, a sympathetic parent allowed them immediate access to her home, where they opened and operated their new school for several weeks until securing a temporary location for their school. The initial school boasted six students' desks and one for the teacher. Within months, a property at 2025 Hillyer Place was secured, and the school's enrollment quickly grew to forty pupils. Five years later, due to Jessie's "remarkable business acumen," determination, and vision, property for another expansion led to the long-time location of the school at 2125 S Street, Washington, D.C. Sadly, for Jessie, her work as the school's leader became a solitary task, after Carolyn Arms suffered a breakdown, resulting in hospitalization and an early demise. Frederick Holton took Carolyn's place as Jessie's unflagging counsel and business advisor.

It is impressive to note that Jessie's vision continues on in the twenty-first century. According to the website of today's, Holton-Arms School, "Mrs. Holton's dream was to create an 'open door' where her students would be inspired to explore new ideas and discover their full potential. She also insisted that they give back to the community." It is evident that this vision continues. Young women in grades three through twelve are served by this college preparatory school, "dedicated to the education not only of the mind, but of the soul and spirit (JMH, 1901)."

Jessie Holton Moon was active in the life of her school until her death at age 85. She was the school's leader for fifty years. She created a business plan to assure that this unique educational institution would carry on successfully after her death. It is a remarkable legacy of an amazing woman that the Holton-Arms School still serves young women 114 years after its creation. Her obituary sums up her life beautifully: "…Her main capital was the force of her own personality. She respected intellectual achievement and she based her school on the idea that young women could learn anything…"

Future generations of educators are well-served by knowing what one woman with a clear vision for potential can accomplish. Jessie Moon Holton's legacy lives on.

B. Ann Lewis Maher

JENNIE C. JONES

was born in Remsen, N.Y. on March 11, 1868 to David W. and Catharine Pritchard Jones. Jennie was one of eight children: William, Simeon, Griffith D., Laura, Ellis D., Sarah (Foust), and Mary (Hughes). Jennie was the third youngest child in the family and remained single. Newspaper articles always referred to her as "Miss Jennie C. Jones."

Jennie was educated in local district schools in Stittville, followed by a business course at Chaffee Shorthand and Business Institute in Oswego, N.Y.

Her brother, Ellis, ran a grocery store in Stittville and Jennie kept his books. Ellis was also postmaster for many years, and Jennie's obituary says she was Deputy Postmaster. Before she moved to Paris Hill, she was employed at the Hurd Shoe Company in Utica.

In 1908, Miss Jennie C. Jones completed special studies at Cornell designed to train extension agents. She became director of Cornell Clubs, the first in Oneida County. Domestic science professors at Cornell University in Ithaca realized many country women could not attend college, but college education could be brought to them. Cornell organized study clubs. Jennie C. Jones was instrumental in organizing Cornell Clubs throughout the state. The clubs later became known as the Home Bureau.

For 25 years, Miss Jones traveled throughout New York state starting clubs in nearly every county. Livingston, Herkimer, Schoharie, Cortland, Chemung, Chenango, Steuben, Monroe and Warren county women, as well as in her own Oneida County, knew and loved Miss Jennie C. Jones.

In 1918, this notice appeared in the Ithaca Daily News: "The morning session is particularly important: Miss Jennie C. Jones will explain what women, organized as home-makers, may hope to accomplish. She is a farm woman whose home is in Paris, N.Y., and has had a great deal of practical experience in meeting the problems of rural women. A vote will be taken after her talk to decide whether Tompkins County women want to form a Home Economics Association – the women's branch of the Farm Bureau."

The Sangerfield Country Club, a Home Bureau unit in Westernville, was organized by Jennie in July 1913. Jennie organized the England Cornell Club in Clinton in October 1915. She organized clubs in Munnsville and in Lowville, N.Y. in 1916. At the Canterbury Hill Chapel in Wright Settlement she organized another club in 1917. In 1919, Jennie organized the Bridgewater unit with ten members, tripling in size during the year. A year later, Jennie was invited to speak at the anniversary party of the Pokonoket Club of Cassville; she also assisted in the founding of this club. Her own Paris Hill Home Bureau was called "Hill Top."

Farmer's wives and rural women lived isolated daily lives; their own chances for socialization came through church groups, Grange Hall meetings and Home Bureau clubs. When Jennie first began her professional career, women were expected to "mind their own business." Their interests and participation in government, public health and community life was not welcomed by the men who thought they were competent to run everything. Jennie was about to change that outlook. Her goal was to bring farm women into an active community, to educate women on basic home living and child raising, and to promote a sense of civic responsibility that would improve their rural lives.

In 1911, she presented a program, "Women as Financiers." She believed that every woman should know about the value of money, the rules of business and how to deal with banks. Every wife should know her husband's financial standing.

A reenactment of 1914 event to show what Jennie Jones and colleagues did.

In May 1914, Miss Jones addressed the Horticultural Society in Butler Hall in New Hartford; her subject, "Ideal Surroundings." "It is an obligation to strive for improvement along horticultural lines in civic and public life," she said. "By improving our surroundings, we elevate the race, the class, and the family, for we become like that with which we associate, and this is true of our physical as well as our mental environment." Clearly, Jennie C. Jones was progressively astute.

Jennie was double-booked as speaker in November 1919 – her fellow speaker was Dr. Ruby Greene Smith, the founder and creator of the Home Bureau creed.

Jennie's speeches stressed the importance for women to have a world outlook. Her speech at the Newark Fair in Wayne County was called "How the Women Can Help Win the War." In 1917, she served as a state food conservation leader making her contribution during World War I. The idea was to voluntarily cut American consumption of food, avoid rationing, and send supplies overseas for our troops. Through the work of conservation leaders such as Jennie, and with promotions such as "Wheatless Wednesday" and "Meatless

Mondays," the effort was successful. American servicemen overseas were fed and a post war famine was lessened.

Miss Jennie Jones organized the Paris Hill Fair in 1907, and served on the board of directors and acted as secretary of the fair for the next 26 consecutive years. Originally the fair began as a fundraiser for the Congregational Church where Jennie was a member. The fair brought the entire rural community together in celebration – farmers exhibiting their best crops, farmers' wives exhibiting jars of canned meats and fruits and homemade dresses, and children grooming pet calves. There were simple games of three-legged races, darning contests, spelling bees, and boys milking contests. The fair was the best place to see the new potato digger in action.

'Something Made from Nothing or Old Clothes Made Into New,' was Miss Jennie's idea in 1919, along with boys' pants made from fathers' coats, and children's dresses made over from old. To draw attraction the first year, the fair offered an automobile ride around the park twice – for a nickel! Some never had been in a car before this! Both dinner and supper meals were offered in the church hall at the cost of 35 cents.

As secretary of the fair, Jennie's duties meant organizing the farmers and their families to be in the proper space at the proper time to stage their equipment and animals; it meant creating new-and-different activities; it meant keeping track of the winners in each category, and seeing that the newspapers were informed. It meant organizing the parade. It meant informing the public of even the smallest details, like this announcement: "Realizing the sanitary importance of the individual drinking cup, we have installed the usual drinking fountain, where paper cups can be bought for one cent each. These can be used more than once by the same individual, and we feel justified."

With her bookkeeping accuracy, Miss Jennie C. Jones kept a list of the contributors that made the fair a success. They included the Honorable Elihu Root of Clinton, the Honorable Charlemagne Tower of Waterville, Sanford Sherman of New Hartford, A.R. Eastman of Waterville, and Thomas R. and Frederick T. Proctor of Utica, to name only a few.

The white Wyandote chickens Jennie raised on her farm were shown at the fair; then received several prizes. Egg production, even during the severe Paris Hill winters, was outstanding; she sold fertilized eggs for hatching in season. Jennie was a member of the National White Wyandote Club.

So great was Jennie's contributions to the Paris Hill Fair that she became known as the Mayor of Paris Hill. Paris Hill received the distinction and honor from Cornell of being a "real fair," without the commercialism and fakery. It was a unique event. Jennie was the force behind the fair, and when she retired due to age, as did many of the older directors, the fair was discontinued after 1938.

By late 1937, Jennie was spending only summers on Paris Hill; she wintered in Utica. Winters are extremely bitter in Paris Hill because of the elevation. Jennie still remained very active and headed a project of installing ten memorial, stained-glass windows in her church on the hill. Also, 1938 found Jennie speaking at the Somerset WCTU on the topic, "Alcohol, a Protoplasmic Poison."

Two different columns for the *Waterville Time* were written by Jennie C. Jones, "The Business of Living" and "Home-Grown Philosophy." They appeared in the 1920s on many occasions.

Jennie was a member of the Paris Hill Grange (from 1895), the Oneida County League of Women Voters, the Oneida County Council on Tuberculosis, the American Country-Life Association, and the Somerset WCTU.

Jennie served as Chaplain of the Ciredwen Lodge of True Ivorites in 1942, keeping with her Welsh heritage.

Jennie C. Jones died on June 25, 1943 at the age of 75. She died in the Old Ladies Home on Faxton Street in Utica. She was survived by her two younger sisters and several nieces and nephews. She is buried in Fairchild Cemetery in Remsen, N.Y.

Janice Trimbey Reilly

HARRIET A. ACKROYD

was born July 28, 1871 in New York Mills, N.Y., the daughter of Joseph and Adelaide Ackroyd. Her father managed the family grocery store in 1893, and in the 1897 City Directory, Joseph was also listed as an undertaker in Yorkville under Ackroyd, Cole (John) and Cash (E.B.). By 1900, the City Directory had the undertaker firm in Utica on Devereux Street, although the Ackroyd residence was still in Yorkville. Harriet grew up in New York Mills with her brother, S. Hoag Ackroyd, who was 11 years younger. She attended Whitestown Seminary, but moved to Utica to graduate from Utica Free Academy. When UFA organized an Alumnae Association in 1903, Harriet got involved, and in 1905 was elected Recording Secretary.

The City Directory of 1893 lists Harriet as Assistant Postmaster in New York Mills. There were also newspaper clippings that reported social activities in which Harriet's name appeared. These clippings provide an insight into what she did. In 1897, Harriet entertained the Cinch Club at her home, and was chairman of Current Topics for the Women's Club of Yorkville. She attended the American Exhibition in Buffalo and was there on September 6, 1901, the day President McKinley was shot.

Harriet remembered being on her grandfather's front porch in Utica when she heard that President Garfield was shot on July 2, 1881, and she was alive when John F. Kennedy was shot on November 22, 1963. Her long and successful life gave her many unique experiences.

In 1907, Harriet was hired by the Utica Fire Insurance Company, a business established three years earlier by 44 businessmen, who started the company by investing $1,000 each. The first two years were very shaky, and at the January 1907 meeting, they discussed closing the company. However the board decided to give it one more try and added a paid staff: a professional insurance man, Fred Homes of New Berlin, N.Y. and Harriet Ackroyd as secretary. Holmes wrote the insurance policies and Harriet kept the books, agent's accounts, made all collections, paid all the bills and took care of the banking. Mr. Holmes was paid $300 plus his compensation from his New Berlin Insurance Company and Harriet was paid $300, with permission to establish her own insurance practice. Mr. Holmes was succeeded by several managers, but Harriet served as a Director and Secretary of the company until 1952, a 45 year commitment. She continued to serve as Director until 1962, when she retired at age 91.

Her manuscript of "A Chronicle of Growth During Our 75 Years 1907-1978," gave a detailed history of her company. Her constant role in directing the company was impressive.

Harriet did establish an insurance company with Cora Farley in 1925 with an office in the Mayro Building. In 1928, she established the Citizens' Casualty Insurance Co., and when Harriet transferred 318 shares of Citizens' Casualty of N.Y. in 1962, the value was $3,539.34.

Besides her obvious success in business world, Harriet made time to be actively involved, in the community. In 1915, she was elected to the newly formed Chamber of Commerce. In 1916, she helped with fundraising for the YWCA and attended the state convention in Rochester. She was Board President in 1927 and 1938, and worked on numerous committees and programs. In 1918, Harriet was active in the Republican Club and worked on the Liberty Loan Committee. She served on the Utica Community Chest (one of six women on the original Board of 21) established in 1918.

In 1919, Harriet was one of the charter members of the Zonta Club of Utica, one of the first nine local clubs in the world. Harriet, as Utica's President, represented the Club when a group of 12 women met to form the National Organization in 1922. In 1923, Harriet was elected National President. She would attend local, state, national and international meetings throughout her life. Records for 2012, show that Zonta is a world-wide organization involving 6,666 women in 555 local chapters in 88 countries.

Harriet was named to the Oneida County Tuberculosis & Health Association, was a vice president, and for five years chaired the annual Christmas Seal Drive. In 1925, Harriet took to the radio waves to address listeners on the new radio station WIBX on the subject of Christmas Seals. In 1931, she represented the chapter at the State Charities Association.

In the 1941 *Builders of Utica*, Harriet was one of only three women in the publication. Her citation reads:

> *"Harriet Augusta Ackroyd: Secretary and Vice President (since 1907) of Utica Fire Insurance Co,: Secretary and Treasurer of Utica Underwriters, Inc.: Secretary, Colonial Fire Insurance Co.: Assistant Secretary and Director, Citizens Casualty of New York: Past President of Zonta International Business and Professional Women: Trustee, New Century Club: Director and Past President of the Young Women's Christian Association; Director, Oneida County Council of Tuberculosis and Public Health: Director of Utica Community Chest: Director, Central School of Nursing: Member, Defense Committee of Oneida County: Member of Trinity Episcopal Church. Educated in Utica Public Schools and Whitestown Seminary: Daughter of the Hon. Joseph and Adelaide Hoag Ackroyd. Business Address: 329 Genesee Street; Home: 42 Grant Street Utica New York."*

In 1942, Harriet served on the Administrative Committee of the Oneida Chapter of the American Red Cross. She headed the Hospital and Recreation Committee responsible for training and placing Grey Ladies at Rhodes General Hospital, which opened in Utica in August 1942 and closed in 1945. Over 300 women took the 24 hour training course and helped throughout the hospital, giving over 1,000 hours of service to the patients at Rhodes Hospital.

Her artistic side was satisfied by being a member of the B Sharp Club (founded in 1903), and she did have her sixty-piece amethyst collection on display at Munson William Proctor Institute in 1940. She delivered speeches to nurses associations, the New York State Association of Hairdressers, as well as programs for Zonta and the YWCA. She was a patron at the dinner where Helen Keller was the speaker at the First Presbyterian Church.

Harriet was always active in her church. She led the Girls Friendly Society of the Episcopal Church. When the National Cathedral in Washington, D.C. was soliciting funds throughout the county, Harriet chaired the local drive. She was active in Republican politics. In 1959, at age 88, she was one of the 2,000 volunteers for Heart Sunday Walk.

Harriet Ackroyd in a photograph taken by Bachrach Studio c. 1950.

Harriet stayed involved with all her organizations until her nineties. She died April 5, 1966 at age 95 at St. Luke's Hospital. Her funeral was at the Trinity Episcopal Church, with burial at Glendale Cemetery in New York Mills. Her will was drawn the year before she died and she left the bulk of her estate of $14,446.16 to her only brother's son, J. Floyd Ackroyd of New Port Richey, Fla., along with his wife, his son and daughter.

Jane Sullivan Spellman

LIBBY SHERMAN KOWALSKY

was born in 1872 in the country of Poland. At age 13 she came to the U.S. by herself to join an adult brother and sister in Utica. She worked in a tailor shop for several years. On January 17, 1892, she married Wolf Kowalsky (1870-1927) who owned a meat market in the second ward, the center of the Jewish community in Utica. He and his parents Mordechai "Max" Kowalsky and Chana "Anna" Prenska Kowalsky had come from Russia to Utica in 1884.

In the 1890 census, Libby is spelt Libbie, and it lists her oldest son as Simon. Their four sons were Herman (Simon in census) (1893 -1950), Louis K. (1894-1967), Morton (Martin in the census) (1899-1959) and Bernard "Spike" (1911 -1979). The family attended Temple Beth El, a congregation that began in 1919.

Libby was described as one of lively spirit and warm of heart. She would have been quite busy as the wife of a businessman and the mother of four young sons. She found the time to take part in these outside organizations: the Ladies Hebrew Aid Society, which began in1908, and would merge in 1915 with the Utica Chapter of the National Council of Jewish Women - a group to help with immigration and naturalization problems; in 1917, the Utica Chapter of Hadassah the Zionist Organization of America, in 1919 the Sisterhood of Temple Beth El and the Jewish Women Service League.

All these organizations did worthwhile things, yet Libby wanted to do 'hands on' helping. In October 1928, the year after her husband died, she, along with Rabbi Albert Dolgroff and Mrs. Jacob Ball, organized the Bikor Cholim Society (society for caring for the sick), whose goal was to visit the Jewish patients in the Utica hospitals. This group saw that every Jewish patient was visited with food, reading material or with personal interaction. Libby was also working with the Jewish Hospital for the Aged in Syracuse, which began in 1912 and served the Utica Area. Libby went to visit the seven or eight Uticans who were patients in Syracuse. She added Marcy State Hospital to her list in 1934. Many times she brought things she knitted or produce from her garden. She and Sister Regina of St. Elizabeth's Hospital became close personal friends, and Libby became a member of the St. Elizabeth's Hospital Guild. She was called Tante Libby.

Libby was one of the four women approved for Chevry Kadishie to prepare Jewish women for burial.

Libby Kowalsky photo taken at family party in 1946.

In 1950, a tea was given in her honor at Temple Beth El and 300 people showed up. Observer Dispatch columnist Alberta Dickinson interviewed her and Libby spoke of her dream for a local home for Jewish men and women. It should be noted that the next year the Charles T. Sitrin Home was established on 13 acres, and a building was purchased by Hyman and Clara Sitrin and sister-in-law Florence R. Sitrin, Charles' widow. The first home had six residents. There have been numerous additions, including a Libby Kowalsky-Wing dedicated in 1974. Today, the Charles T. Sitrin Health Care Center is a large complex institution that has pioneered many health care services, including the convalescent care Libby wanted.

In August of 1958, at age 86, a "Tante Libby Day" was declared and she received a letter from President Dwight Eisenhower commending her on her many charitable contributions.

She was to use Sitrin's services before she died on October 21, 1959. She is buried in House of Israel Cemetery on Wood Road. Two sons, Herman and Morton, predeceased her, but she had her remaining sons, three daughters-in-law, seven grandchildren and three great-grandchildren, as well as legions of friends, to mourn her.

In 1916 her sons continued her tradition of giving. Morton and Louis would begin their working life by establishing what is today Empire Recycling, one of the largest recycling centers in New York State. Her son, Bernard, always known as "Spike," with his wife Betty Kamino Kowalsky, established the first family discount store in the Utica area when they opened State Street Mill in 1963. Spike would be on hand to dedicate the North Wing at the Charles T. Sitrin Home as the Libby Kowalsky Wing in 1974. Her dream really did come true.

Jane Sullivan Spellman

WELTHY HONSINGER FISHER

was born on September 18, 1879, the daughter of Abram Walker Honsinger, an iron forger, and his second wife, Welthy Blakesley Sanford, a teacher. They had five children: a son who died in infancy, Fred, Mabel, Mina, and Welthy, her father's most beloved child.

She idolized her father who was a great influence and stabilizing force in her life. At the age of 10, she was captivated and inspired by her second idol, Nellie Bly (1865-1922), a journalist who traveled around the world demanding reforms and focusing on the poor treatment of women. She told her mother she wanted to do the same. In 7th grade, she wrote an essay about Nellie Bly, which was her first published work for the Rome Sentinel.

Welthy graduated in 1896 from Rome Free Academy and studied music at Syracuse University, receiving her bachelor's degree in 1900. She went on to study music in New York City, with aspirations of becoming an opera singer. She supported herself by teaching school in Haverstraw, N.Y. and Englewood, N.J.

In 1906, she had a life-changing experience after listening to Robert Speer, a missionary, speak in Carnegie Hall, making a plea for young people to go and help others around the world. She decided to travel to China as a Methodist missionary and became headmistress of Bao Lin, a girls' school in Nanchang Province serving from 1906-1918. In 1911, when the school was destroyed by fire, she returned to the U.S. to raise money for a new building. In China, she encouraged girls to develop into modern Chinese women, often against the wishes of their traditional parents. The sign hanging over the school gate read, "Ye shall know the truth and the truth shall make you free." She appointed a Chinese woman to be second in authority, which marked the first time a Chinese woman was ever a critical force in a missionary school. Being committed to the idea of women's independence, she knew if she could give them the tools they needed through education, they could change China. Her motto, a Chinese proverb, was the guiding force of her own life; "It is better to light one candle than to curse the darkness."

During World War I, she worked for the YWCA in England and France, and lectured in the U.S. on women of the Allies.

The next great event of her life, at age 44, was her marriage to Frederick Bohn Fisher (1882-1938) in 1924, a Methodist bishop in India and Burma who shared her similar beliefs for India and the future. She was ready at a moment's notice to speak, campaign, raise money, or travel for the people she helped in India. Together, they worked for cooperation among all peoples and cultures in order to eradicate suffering and to promote world peace. During their travels, they realized that the lack of education and poverty was the cause of much suffering in the world, and both spoke publicly in the U.S. to raise this awareness. Despite dedication to their Christian beliefs, they embraced all religions equally, and felt that people could not afford to let religious differences put up walls between them. This drew the attention of Mahatma Gandhi (1869-1948) who became a friend and inspiration to her. Gandhi's dedication and self-sacrifice impressed Welthy. The Fishers engaged in conversations with him on how best to solve India's problems.

After her husband's sudden death in 1938, she once again continued her life's work, traveling widely to China and India as a journalist, and to South America and the Middle East studying women and educational systems. In 1947, six weeks before his death, Gandhi asked her to return to India permanently to continue her work in education for India's villages. Believing that literacy was, beyond all doubt, the key to helping women and all people advance, become independent, and move away from poverty to a "New India," she did return in 1952 and dedicated herself to the cause of starting a literacy movement.

In 1953, at the age of 74, she started Literacy House, a small informal school combining literacy with agricultural training in Allaabad, India, which was moved to Luckhow in 1956. It became a complete village of learning, with dorms, classrooms, a library, and a House of Prayer for all people, offering teacher training for about 450 teachers a year. Literacy House today plays a key role in the government of India's program to make 100 million young people literate. Welthy became known as "Lady Literacy." In 1967, she introduced puppets into her programs, as puppets were accepted by the students universally as representations of no particular religion, caste, or race.

Welthy Fisher picture taken in 1956 at the inauguration of the Literacy House in India.

Not long after, Welthy and other literacy pioneers realized that the "New India" concept could expand to other areas of the world as well. World Education was formed in New York City and dedicated to providing literacy training to those who most needed it throughout the world. She also helped start another non-profit; World Literacy of Canada in Toronto in 1955. She was deeply involved with both, either as president or as an advisor from 1951 to 1972, when she gave up her official duties. Thanks to her tireless efforts, World Education continues to carry on her work into the 21st century, reaching large numbers of people today.

At the age of 93, she once again traveled freely, visiting China in 1973. Welthy returned to Peking at the age of 98, as the oldest foreign guest to China, and met Mme. Sun Yat-Sen. She made farewell visits to India in 1973, 1977, with the last being in 1980. Quoting Welthy, "I could never be bothered about chronological age. I've been too busy trying to get things done," was indicative of her amazing energy that persisted until the day she died of old age on December 16, 1980 in Southbury, Connecticut. She was 101.

Welthy was the recipient of hundreds of honors and awards. She received an honorary doctorate from Syracuse University, her alma mater. In 1978, she was a nominee for a UNESCO award for contributing to world literacy. The Indian government honored her literacy work by issuing a commemorative postage stamp in her likeness on March 18, 1980, the only American honored in this manner. Her work was highlighted in *Time* magazine in a 1966 article titled "Education Abroad: India's Literacy Lady." She wrote numerous books, including her husband's biography, *Frederick Bohn Fisher-World Citizen* in 1944, and her own autobiography, *To Light a Candle,* in 1962.

In November 1998, a state historical marker was placed at 307 West Court Street in Rome, N.Y., where Welthy was born and raised.

Susan Guzik Tice

GRACE VAN WAGENEN CARPENTER

was born on February 26, 1880, in Oxford, Chenango County, New York. She was the daughter of William Hubert Van Wagenen (1837-1917) and Anna L. Selden (1850-1940). Grace was the middle child of William and Anna's three daughters. Her older sister, Louise Van Wagenen, was born in 1877 and later married Harry W. Libby. Younger sister, Nellie Van Wagenen, was born in 1881 and was later married to Clarence Rufus Keeney.

Grace's father, William Van Wagenen, was born in Oxford, New York. He was the son of John and Sarah Ann Hopkins Van Wagenen, and grandson of Revolutionary War veteran, Garrit H. Van Wagenan. For 30 years, he engaged in the pharmaceutical business in Oxford. He was a charter member of the Board of Directors of the First National Bank of Oxford, where he was elected vice president in 1911. On Jan. 21, 1874, he married Miss Anna L. Selden of Williamstown, Oswego Co. N.Y. William moved his family to Rome, N.Y., in 1887, where he was a member of the Selden & Van Wagenen lumber firm. He died in 1917 following surgery. A tribute published after his death stated that no one "...was more popular and so generally liked..."

Grace's mother, Anna L. Selden Van Wagenen was born at Williamstown, the daughter of Jacob and Sarah Jane Bunn Selden. As a young girl she attended Miss Whittamore's school in Rome. After her marriage, she lived with her husband in Oxford. Upon her return to Rome in 1888, she held the office of secretary for the Girls' Friendly Society of the Zion Episcopal Church for 25 years. She was a founding member of the Rome Civic Improvement Society and a charter member of the Wednesday Morning Club, The Women's Club and the board of the Rome Home (an adult care facility). She was also affiliated with the Rome Girl Scout Council and the Oak Twig (a women's volunteer service organization). She was an active church member and civic worker until her death in 1940 at the age of 90.

Grace Van Wagenen attended school in Rome and graduated from Rome Free Academy. In 1902, she married Arthur Fuller Carpenter. Arthur Carpenter (1874-1943) was a native Roman, son of Erwin C. and Julia Fuller Carpenter. He attended Rome Free Academy, Warington Classical School in Washington, D.C., and graduated from Yale with the class of 1895. After his graduation, he worked for a short time in Boston and Maryland before return-ing to Rome to serve as secretary and

Grace Carpenter in photo c. 1897.

treasurer of the Rome Metallic Bedstead Company from 1900 to 1924 and as president from 1924, until his retirement in 1933. Arthur served as a trustee of the Rome Library Association and he conducted seminars in the School of Related Arts and Sciences (New York City and Utica). He was a member of the Rome Chamber of Commerce and worshiped with his wife at the Zion Episcopal Church.

In 1923, Grace's wish for a "house that Jane Austen would have lived in" was fulfilled when the couple created their magnificent Tudor style home on West Bloomfield Street in Rome. She and her husband were personally in-volved in every aspect of designing the house, decorating and furnishing each room. Grace's art studio occupied the third floor where, in addition to painting and sculpture, she authored two books of poetry: *"Friends of the Road,"* pub-lished in 1932, and *"The Besieging Spirit,"* published in 1936.

Grace was active in many youth, community and religious organizations, and often opened her home as a meeting place for these groups. In 1911, she was elected president of the Rome Civic Improvement Association. In the 1920s, Grace's hosted The Harmony Club, a music appreciation group that presented guest musicians. Her sister, Louise, was the president. Grace was also active in the Wednesday Morning Club, started in 1892, a group of 40 like-minded women who were described as "starving for real, regular mental food." She served on the education and youth commissions of the Episcopal Diocese of Central New York, and assisted in establishing St. Andrew's Episcopal Mission Church at Lake Delta. She was one of the co-founders of the Women's Community Center that later merged with the Rome YMCA, now the Rome Family Y.

In 1943, Grace lost her husband, Arthur, to a bacterial infection following surgery. Since they had no children, all their property, including their unique home, belonged entirely to Grace. She continued to use her home and assets to support the arts and organizations she valued so highly.

Grace lived out her last days in her lovely home where she died on March 9, 1966, after a long illness. In her will, Grace left bequests to her sisters and nephew, as well as several other individuals and institutions. Continuing her philanthropy, she left bequests locally to Jervis Library, the Zion Episcopal Church, The Women's General Study Club, and the Home for Aged Women in Rome. The Parochial Fund of the Central New York Diocese of the Protestant Episcopal Church in Syracuse also received a bequest. In New York City, her generosity extended to the Episcopal Church Fund and to The Andrew Freedman Home, which was a New York City retirement home for elderly people who had lost their fortunes. A portrait of Bishop Lloyd was gifted to the Episcopal Cathedral of St. John the Divine, in New York City.

The Carpenter Home was purchased by the City of Rome and in 1967 it became the Rome Art and Community Center, fulfilling Grace's wish that her home provide a local setting to foster the arts with accommodations for classes and exhibits.

In 2007, Grace Van Wagenen Carpenter was inducted into the Rome Arts Hall of Fame, which annually awards six inductions to persons who have made a major contribution to the arts in the Rome community. She is considered to be Rome's first patron of the arts.

Roberta Seaton Walsh

ZAIDA ZOLLER

was born in Little Falls, N.Y. on July 22, 1882 to Jacob (1833-1907) and Mary Jane Dygert (1842-1930) Zoller. She had a twin brother Abram (1882-1962) and three older siblings John (1873-1964), Maude (1876-1962), and Thomas (1878-1952). At an early age, she showed signs of leadership accepting the role of president of a Literary Society for 7th and 8th grade girls at the Church Street School in Little Falls. She continued her education at the Mary A. Burnham School in North Hampton, Massachusetts, to prepare girls for further learning and graduated from Miss Hewitt's School in New York City in the class of 1902.

Zaida came from an enterprising family. Her father Jacob was a successful businessman in Little Falls, whose company, the Zoller Packing House, manufactured and distributed cheese, beef and pork products, butter and eggs. He served on four bank boards and owned nine dairy farms in Herkimer and Montgomery counties. Zaida's two older brothers, John and Thomas, followed in their father's footsteps as successful businessmen. John assisted with the family company and other business ventures - C.J. Lundstrom and Valley Mills companies. Thomas was organizer and director of the Standard Bookcase Company and the Hall Incubating Company. Her sister, Maude, actively supported the Little Falls Hospital as president of the Hospital Board for many years, and Zaida's, twin, Abram, was Little Falls mayor (1916-1920), Herkimer County Judge (1929-1933), and Supreme Court Justice (1934-1952).

Zaida was a woman of influence in her own right. Early on she took an interest in her father's farms and managed several of them after her father's death. She is best remembered for her love of animals and mobilized the advancement of animal welfare in the area as one of the lead founders of Herkimer County's first Humane Society in 1913. A family story relates her stopping a traveling circus that came to Little Falls in 1912 to address neglect of the animals and to make sure they were given good care. She was appointed as a Humane Officer of Little Falls and acted as the Humane Society's volunteer investigator with the authority to make arrests for cruelty to animals. She led the Herkimer County Humane Society as its pres-

Zaida Zoller portrait made from photo taken in 1907

ident for 40 years, stepping down in 1963, but remaining as its honorary president until her death in 1980. Under her directorship, several shelter facilities to house the animals were established in Ilion, Getman Corners, Middleville, and eventually in 1962, at Fort Herkimer where it is located today. Her legacy is carried on today by an active Humane Society where her portrait is housed to continue to watch over its dealings.

While Zaida was actively involved with the animal welfare movement, she was also concerned with matters benefiting the general welfare of the community, from standing up for women's rights with the suffrage movement, to promoting public health. As an educated woman who effected change in her community, women's suffrage was a leading priority for Zaida. In 1917, when suffrage leaders were rallying at a state convention in Saratoga, Zaida, as chairman of the Little Falls Suffrage Party, hosted the women en route at an outdoor meeting in Little Falls. That same year, she was chairman for a suffrage mass meeting in Little Falls, inviting the honorary chairman of the

National Woman Suffrage Association as its speaker, Dr. Ann Howard Shaw (1847-1919). Women in New York State were allowed to vote in 1917, and after the 19th Amendment to the United States Constitution granted all women the right to vote in 1920, Zaida recognized the importance of this tremendous achievement and headed up the Herkimer County Branch of the League of Women Voters urging women to vote and instruct them in political affairs.

In the midst of caring for animals and striving for the right to vote, Zaida was actively involved with the Red Cross. In 1918, she headed up the Red Cross Ladies Canteen Service committee, which supplied lunches to the young military men leaving for their army camps and suppers to army truckmen traveling through the city of Little Falls. A year later, after the close of World War I, she helped welcome the returning soldiers back home as a member of the Little Falls Welcome Home Committee. In 1921, she became chairman of the nursing activities of the Red Cross Chapter in Little Falls, to sponsor a nursing service to go out into the community to help "the unfortunate, teaching the gospel of clean living and well being," according to a *Journal and Courier* article of December 6, 1921.

Zaida worked to promote public health on the governmental level when, in 1919, she became a member and secretary of the Little Falls Health Co-Ordination Committee that was organized by the State Department of Health. The committee's objective was to create a health center to coordinate health activities in one building, bringing together support for the health officer and local board of health. Zaida recognized the vital need for access to health care as paramount because of an influenza epidemic sweeping the nation and the large number of factory workers living on low wages and in poor conditions in the city. According to a 1912 New York State Department of Labor Report, Little Falls had a total of 50 factories and 3,876 employees.

Zaida also actively served on the Herkimer County Tuberculosis Committee and served as its secretary in 1920 when Pine Crest Sanatorium in Salisbury, a new facility to treat tuberculosis patients, opened. She continued her support of the facility by participating in Christmas Seal campaigns to raise funds for the center.

She appreciated her historical heritage and was a member of the Asten-rogen Chapter of the D.A.R. and was named its chapter Regent from 1950-1952. Zaida descended from Jacob Zoller (1741-1777), who served under Col. Campbell and Ebenezer Cox in the American Revolution and died from his wounds at the Battle of Oriskany.

Her church was very important to her and she was a faithful attendant at the St. Paul's Universalist Church, serving as a Sunday School teacher, on the Church Board of Trustees, and was involved with the Women's National Missionary Association and the Women's Christian Association.

Her many contributions to the community were acknowledged when she was awarded the Staff Sergeant Steve Stefula Post #4612 Little Falls V.F.W. Citizenship Award in 1957, a life dedicated to helping the less fortunate and making the world a better place in which to live.

Zaida Zoller died January 22, 1980 at the age of 98 in the house in which she was born – the handsome home her father built in 1876, which still stands in Little Falls. She is buried in Fairview Cemetery nearby.

The objectives of the many organizations that Zaida Zoller devoted her time and efforts to, reflected her inherent values as a humanitarian – to be of help to the unfortunate, to promote the general health of the community, and in her own words as she was rallying for the local branch of the League of Women Voters in 1922, "urging to get behind the welfare and humane projects that tend to elevate and benefit the public welfare."

Caryl Darling Hopson

ADELAIDE THOMPSON WILLIAMS WHITE

was born September 1864 in Dunkirk, Chautauqua County, N.Y., the fifth child and third daughter of Dr. Julian T. Williams and Julia King Thompson. Adelaide's grandparents, Dr. Ezra and Sarah King Clarke Williams, had left Oneida County, N.Y. in 1820, intending to move west to Sandusky, Ohio. But when they arrived at Dunkirk (a stopping point for lake boats), Dr. Williams was so impressed with the area that they stopped there, becoming one of the earliest pioneer families of Chautauqua County.

Adelaide's father, Dr. Julian Taintor Williams, was the eighth child of Ezra and Sarah Williams. He was born in Dunkirk, N.Y. in 1828 and died there in 1905. After graduating from medical school, he practiced medicine and sold pharmaceuticals. In 1882, he bought the Dunkirk Printing Company and became the publisher of several newspapers. He was on the Dunkirk Board of Education for almost fifty years. He served two terms on the New York State Assembly and, in 1887, he was elected supervisor to represent Dunkirk on the County Board, serving until 1891. He married Adelaide's mother, Julia King Thompson, in Dunkirk on December 15, 1851.

Adelaide's three sisters were Henrietta Clark Williams, Jessie Carlisle Williams, and Geraldine Williams. Her oldest sister, Henrietta, was born almost ten years before Adelaide, in 1853. She married Walter Scott, of Philadelphia and had three children. Jessie was born in 1858, graduated from Vassar College, married Charles Watson Hinkley of Chicago and had one child. Another sister, Geraldine, was born in 1860 and died in 1867.

Adelaide's oldest brother, Henry Kirk Williams, was born in 1856, attended Cornell University, married May Elizabeth Willis and had five children. He eventually became president and general manager of the Dunkirk Printing

Company. Adelaide's younger brother, Gerald Bismarck Williams, was born in 1870. At the age of nineteen he began working for his father's company, Dunkirk Printing, and eventually became the editor of the *Dunkirk Evening Observer.* He married Elizabeth MacLeod of Louisville, Kentucky.

Adelaide Williams attended Dunkirk Union schools and followed her sister Jessie to Vassar College.

Adelaide was married on November 12, 1904, to Dr. Harry Draper White, a medical doctor and president of the staff of Rome Hospital. He was the son of Henry Kirke White and Mary Bullard Draper. Dr. and Mrs. White were the parents of one daughter, Julia Kirke White. Julia attended the Birmingham School and Pine Manor Junior College. In 1941, she married John Hathaway Dyett, who was vice president of the Rome Cable Corporation. They had three grandchildren: Herbert Thomas, daughter Kirke VanArman and John Hathaway.

In 1913, the National Woman's Party was founded by women's rights activists, Alice Paul and Lucy Burns, to fight for women's suffrage. It had broken off from the much larger National American Woman Suffrage Association over a disagreement about the Shafroth-Palmer Amendment. That amendment would require any state with more than 8 percent signing an initiative petition, to hold a state referendum on suffrage. Paul and Burns felt that this amendment was a lethal distraction from their ultimate goal of an all-encompassing federal amendment protecting the rights of all American women.

Adelaide White is on a bronze Suffrage Memorial tablet listing the names of
100 N.Y. women placed in Capitol in Albany c. 1920

Three area women helped solicit money for the National Women's Party: Lucy Carlile Watson, founder of the Utica Political Equality Club, Glendolyn Bens, also of Utica, and Adelaide Williams White. Although they did not picket, they were part of a 50-member area women's group supporting Alice Paul and her efforts to secure the vote.

The September 1, 1914, issue of the *Rome Daily Sentinel* reported that the Political Equality Club of Rome, N.Y., held its first meeting the previous day. Adelaide Williams White was the first president of the local organization. At that first meeting the group decided to extend an invitation to Miss Helen M. Todd to speak to the group. Miss Todd was the author of *"Getting Out the Vote"* and a very dynamic and popular speaker on women's suffrage. It was significant that she came from San Francisco because she had actually voted in a state election. Three years earlier, California had passed Amendment 8, granting women the right to vote in state elections almost a decade before the 19th Amendment provided women's suffrage throughout the United States. There was extensive newspaper coverage of Miss Todd's appearances at the Oneida County Fair in Boonville and at the New York State Fair in Syracuse. The following year, still under Adelaide's administration, the Political Equality Club's invited speaker was Mrs. A. C. Hughston, the New York organizer for the Empire State Suffragist Campaign Committee.

Adelaide Thompson Williams White died at age 53 on July 7, 1917. Services were held first at her home at 217 West Embargo Street in Rome. Her family then accompanied her body on the train to Dunkirk, where a simple service was held at the home of her older brother, Henry. Burial followed in the family lot at Forest Hill Cemetery in Fredonia, N.Y.

After Adelaide's death, Dr. White married for a second time on October 29, 1918, to Marion Beecher Fear, and they became the parents of two children, Jessie B. (White) Henze and Harry D. White.

Roberta Seaton Walsh

DR. LAURA FRANCES BROOKS-HARNEY

was born in Schroon Lake, Essex County, N.Y. on February 7, 1885. She was the daughter of Smith W. Brooks and Philomena St. Martin-Brooks. A brother, Frederick, was born in September 1887. Smith Brooks had once attended law school but operated a dairy farm when Laura was born. When her mother, Philomena, died of tuberculosis in 1892, Smith moved back to his family's Schroon Lake homestead so his widowed mother, Laura A. Brooks, could help with the children.

After graduating from high school, Laura took a teachers' examination in Warrensburg, N.Y. in 1903 and taught briefly at a school near Schroon Lake. She accepted a position in 1905 at the one-room Moose River Settlement School ten miles from Boonville, N.Y. in northern Oneida County. Over the next forty years, she earned a permanent teaching certificate at Potsdam State Normal School, a physical education certificate at Syracuse, and three degrees from New York University: a Bachelor of Science in 1928, a Masters of Arts in 1931 and a Doctor of Education in 1939. She also obtained a Bachelor of Library Science degree from Albany State College in 1937, and did postgraduate studies at Harvard.

While teaching at the Moose River Settlement, Laura met Patrick J. Harney, a bookkeeper and partner in the Wood, Harney & Foley Supply Store at Fulton Chain. The mill town was located two miles south of Old Forge in northern Herkimer County and was the railroad station gateway to the scenic Fulton Chain of Lakes region. As a member of the school board, Patrick recruited Laura in 1906 to teach grades one through eighth in the schoolhouse at Fulton Chain for $13 per week. In her classroom were more than 50 pupils, primarily from first-generation Irish, German, Polish, and French Canadian lumberjack and millworker families.

On June 30, 1907, Laura married Patrick J. Harney and they took up residence at Van Auken's Hotel next to the railway station. Laura looked after the three Van Auken children to help pay for their room and board. Their first child, Patrick J. Harney Jr., was born in June 1908. Two years later, her husband sold out his store interest at Fulton Chain to Patrick J. Foley. The Harney family lived for a short time in Syracuse and operated an egg business. Laura took in roomers. Their second child, James E. Harney, was born there in 1912.

When it became obvious that Patrick's health was failing due to diabetes and he could not provide for the family, Laura returned to teaching. She accepted a position at a one-room schoolhouse at Carter Station, another lumber town just outside of Old Forge. She and her children lived in a shack, hiring a fourth grader to watch young James. In the fall of 1913, the family reunited at Fulton Chain when Patrick found work as a bookkeeper. Laura taught at a temporary school in the Town Hall while a new school was being built.

Family health problems were a constant source of anguish for Laura Harney. In January 1911, she hastened down to Columbia College in New York City to escort her brother, Frederick, home to Schroon Lake. He had long suffered from tuberculosis and succumbed to the disease at the age of 24 at the Brooks' homestead in mid-February. The year 1917 was particularly devastating. Grandma Laura Brooks died in January at Schroon Lake of tuberculosis, hastened by influenza. While attending her funeral, Laura was called home when her son Patrick Jr. also got influenza and her husband had pneumonia. A neighbor and nurse, Katie Morse, helped Laura who was nearly overwhelmed with responsibilities. To add to the horror, her four-year old son, James, contracted typhoid fever and died on January 27, 1918. Without a cemetery in Old Forge, his body was taken to St. Joseph's Cemetery in Boonville for burial.

Laura's career took on added importance for the economic welfare of the family. In 1918, she resigned as principal of the new Fulton Chain School and accepted a teaching position in Tupper Lake for two years and then coached and taught physical education in New Hartford, N.Y. from 1920 to 1924. Her relationship with her husband waned after the death of their son James, and to their apparent incompatibility yet Laura would wear her wedding ring for the remainder of her married life.

Patrick Sr., Laura, and Patrick Jr. Harney are listed in the 1925 Census for Old Forge, living in a home on Garmon Avenue that Laura would return to for the next 45 years. She taught physical education in Boonville, N.Y. in 1925-1926 while her son completed his studies at the Town of Webb School. As his health permitted, Patrick Harney Sr. worked in real estate and sold insurance. He continued to battle with diabetes, but succumbed to the disease at the age of 59 on September 3, 1932.

From 1926-1946, Laura Brooks-Harney spent the school year in West-chester County teaching science and mathematics at Washington Jr. High School and as the principal of Pennington Elementary School in Mount Vernon, N.Y. The proximity to Albany and New York City allowed her to complete three advanced degrees. The thesis for her Doctor of Education degree at New York University was based on two summers of research at the Matanuska Colony in Alaska.

Laura Harney in a photo taken c. 1930.

In 1928, at the age of 43, Laura began taking flying lessons at the Curtiss Airport at Valley Stream, Long Island. On the 3rd of February 1930, she successfully passed her tests and became the 134th woman in the United States to obtain a private pilot's license. The course covered airplane and engine inspection, navigation, meteorology, and 30 hours of supervised flight time. In 1932, she competed in a two-day flying derby from Curtiss-Wright Airport to Atlantic City, along with three other women fliers and fifteen men. Mrs. Harney won the spot landing award. That same year, she published, "The Skycraft Book," a history of flying, a result of her Master's thesis. She became the 37th member to join a group of all women flyers called the Ninety-Nines. Amelia Earhart, a personal friend, was the first president of the organization, which is still in existence today.

Dr. Harney applied for a U.S. Foreign Service position in 1946 and spent 26 months teaching adult education in post-war Germany. After a brief visit home, she was off to teach at an American school in Rio de Janeiro, Brazil, for a year. During the early 1950s, she served as a Cultural Affairs Officer/Attaché with the Education Office of the US Embassy in Karachi, Pakistan. In 1953, she was offered an English teacher-position at the State College at Frostburg College, Maryland. For the next seven years, she was a member of the school's faculty and also worked in the departments of guidance, public relations, and recruitment.

At the age of 75 in 1960, Laura returned to her beloved home on Garmon Avenue in Old Forge. During the next decade, she operated a Curio Shop in the middle of town and sold imported items from around the world. She served as Executive Secretary of the Central Adirondack Association in Old Forge and was frequently requested to lecture on education and her travels to many groups throughout the region. In the mid-1960s, Laura went out on the lecture circuit to support Barry Goldwater's campaign during his run for the presidency.

Always the educator and a legend in her community, Dr. Harney welcomed hundreds of local students into her home to view the collectibles she had acquired from around the world. A favorite tradition she established was hosting an annual graduation party at her house for Town of Webb High School Seniors.

Dr. Laura Brooks-Harney spent the last decade of her life with her son Patrick J. Harney Jr., at their home on Sunnyside Drive, New Hartford, N.Y. Patrick had retired after a successful career as a research engineer, an airline dispatcher, radar operator and meteorologist with United Airlines and the U.S. Air Force. Still agile and interested in foreign travel in her nineties, she went on a safari trip to Africa. Dr. Harney died after a short illness in May 1981 at the age 96 at St. Elizabeth's Hospital in Utica and was buried with her husband Patrick J. Harney and son James E. Harney at St. Joseph's Cemetery in Boonville, N.Y.

In 1986, a granite marker inscribed with Dr. Laura Harney's name was added to the International Forest of Friendship in Atchison, Kansas, the birthplace of Amelia Earhart, in a memorial park for the Ninety-Niners women aviators and other aeronautics and aviation notables. A Dr. Laura Harney academic scholarship fund was established in 1981 to benefit a Town of Webb High School senior planning to attend college. Since the death of Patrick J. Harney Jr. in 2001, the scholarship is awarded annually in memory both Dr. Harney and her son in honor of their lifelong value of the merits of a higher education.

Peg Nash Masters

GRACE MCCLURE DIXON
COGSWELL ROOT

was born in 1890, the daughter of Ledyard Cogswell (1852-1929) and Cornelia McClure (1855-1908) Cogswell of Albany, N.Y. Grace was raised by a busy father, her older sister Cornelia (1880-1972) and brother Ledyard Cogswell, Jr. (1878), a successful businessman in Albany. Grace had a lonely childhood, not challenged at the Albany schools and two boarding schools she attended. She always lamented never going to college. Tall and energetic, Grace did well in sports.

At age 26, Grace was admitted to a Catskill sanitarium to recover from a horseback riding accident. There she met 32-year-old Edward Wales Root (1884-1956) the youngest son of the internationally known Elihu Root (1845-1937) and his wife Clara Wales Root (1855-1928). Edward had an older sister, Edith (1873-1962) and brother Elihu Root IV (1881-1967). At age three Edward had mastoiditis and lost most of his hearing. His mother told him to ignore his deafness and he withdrew from most social situations. He did graduate (Phi Beta Kappa) from Hamilton College, in 1905 and held several jobs including one which involved traveling with his father to South America in 1906. He did work for the *New York Sun* where he covered art galleries. Many of his friends were artists and he was involved in the Armory Show in 1913. Edward purchased his friends' works because they needed money and he chose well. His collection of early 20th-century paintings was outstanding. Edward had entered the sanitarium following a physical breakdown.

Grace and Edward were wonderful for each other. They took long walks and shared their interest in books, paintings, and nature. They were married September 8, 1917 in the Rose Garden of the bride's sister, Cornelia, and her husband, N.Y. State Senator Henry N. Sage (1868- 1933) in Menands, N.Y.

Grace's uncle, the Rev. Dr. James G. K. McClure of Lake Forest Ill, performed the ceremony. Grace's niece, Cornelia Cogswell Sage, age six, was her only attendant and Major Ulysses S. Grant, Edward's brother-in-law was his best man. The honeymoon was in the Canadian Rockies and their first home address was 1215 16th Street, Washington, D.C.

Their first permanent home was the homestead on the Hamilton College Campus where Edward began his 20 years as lecturer of art. In the early 1920s, Edward and Grace traveled with his father on international assignments.

Their only son, John, was born September 2, 1922 and Grace would start working on *Father and Daughter, Letters of Mason Fitch Cogswell* (1761-1830) which she edited and published in 1924. She also began a fern garden in the family Root Garden behind her home.

In 1929, Grace began to work with Pauline Sabin on the Women's Organization for National Prohibition Reform (WONPR), organized May 28 with the sole purpose of repealing the 18th amendment (effective Jan. 16, 1920). This group of women became impatient with the work the men's groups were doing to repeal the laws which they felt had resulted in a nationwide crime wave and was not a cure for the evils of alcohol. Grace would write *The History of the WONPR,* published in 1933, that would provide the names of women who led this organization. There were no dues and the women paid their way to the National Convention held April 23, 1930 in Cleveland, Ohio, reporting 100,000 members. By the February 2, 1931 convention in Washington, D.C. there were 330,000 members; the third convention had 620,000 and by election time in 1932, 1,326,862 were enrolled. It should be noted that many of the WONPR were active Republicans who could not get Herbert Hoover's support for the repeal and therefore voted for Franklin Roosevelt, who did support the repeal. Once the 28th amendment was passed, WONPR voted itself out of business. Grace's 217-page book is a fascinating record of what these women accomplished.

During the 1930s, Grace worked with Philip Jessup, a 1920 Hamilton College graduate who wrote a two-volume biography of Elihu Root published in 1937, the year Elihu Root died. Her own book "Four Sons," a two-volume explanation of the Root Family and Hamilton College was published in 1942.

In 1952, for the first time in Hamilton College history, honorary degrees were given to a husband and wife. Grace was given a Masters of Humane Letters. Grace's citation said:

> *"On this hilltop students often think masculinity holds too exclusive sway, it is fitting that honor be paid to Grace Cogswell Root whose gracious influence upon this community has been as continuing as it had been unselfish. Keen-minded and talented, her wide civic, charitable and intellectual interests have long added luster to the life of the college community. Many undergraduates have known her as a generous and gifted hostess. Her characteristic enthusiasm for Hamilton and for its well being has been a constant. Her contributions have been many to the cultural enrichment not only of the college but of the neighboring communities as well. It was indeed a fortunate day for Hamilton when she came to make her home upon our hill."*

Grace Root photo taken from Edmund Wilson's Upstate N.Y. Home in 1971.

When Edward died December 5, 1956, Grace established the Root Glen Foundation to support the wonderful garden started by her husband's grandfather, Oren Root (1803-1885) in 1850, when he bought the old 1812 structure and made it a home with his wife Nancy Buttrick Root (1812-1891). Oren's son Elihu, took an interest in the garden now named "The Glen". Grace would expand Edward's studio built on the property and used this as her Hamilton home until her death. Their home became the Root Art Gallery. In 1962 she deeded the 20-acre Root Glen to the Root Glen Foundation attached to Hamilton College, working hard to extend the educational programs in this area. Grace would dissolve the Foundation in 1971, when she gave the Root Glen to Hamilton College.

Grace was much in favor of the establishing Kirkland College in 1968. Kirkland was across the street from Hamilton and was for women. She served as a trustee and was proud of the many new educational ideas the new college would institute.

Grace spent her winters in New York City and belonged to the Cosmopolitan Club. She died February 3, 1975, age 84 after a brief illness. Her funeral was held at the Hamilton College Chapel, and her friend Silvia Saunders quoted from "Grace's Sheet of Instructions": "After three score and ten (which I have already exceeded) I feel there should be a celebration over death instead of mourning. For me, this celebration should not be indoors. And I have known all the weathers that have existed on the Hill."

Grace was survived by her son John, his wife Naida Bourauni Root and their daughter Melinda. She is buried in the Hamilton College Cemetery where her husband is buried, as well as her son John, upon his death July 9, 2010.

Jane Sullivan Spellman

HELENE CHADWICK

was born November 25, 1897 in Chadwicks, N.Y. to George W. Chadwick, Jr. and Marie Louise Norton. Marie was an opera singer and actress and we shall soon see her daughter followed in her footsteps to be on stage years later. Helene had one younger sister, Marguerite, who married a poor barber from New York City by the name of Mauri Maffucci. Marguerite died at the age of 33 in 1924.

Helen Chadwick's great-grandparents were the founders of the present hamlet of Chadwicks, N.Y., located in the Town of New Hartford – Washington Mills being to the north and Sauquoit to the south. John and Betsey Snow Chadwick hailed from Oldham, Lancashire, England. John was the founder of the Eagle Mills, a cotton factory located along Sauquoit Creek. Following a return trip to England, John installed large wooden engraved blocks, which were used in printing calicoes. He was one of the foremost pioneer textile manufacturers of the Sauquoit Valley.

Helene spent her childhood days growing up in the three-story Chadwick house on Elm Street, built in 1881. A playhouse in the backyard might have served as her stage for imaginary plays. The Chadwick stately mansion was across the road from the Standard Silk Mill; the house burned in a devastating fire in 1962.

Helene's early education took place in a one-room schoolhouse built on mill property and located on Elm Street between the railroad depot and the silk mill. A larger schoolhouse was built around 1907 and stood on School Street in the same area. It was common practice for owners of large mills to provide schools, churches, stores and small houses to rent to their workers – as sort of compensation to remain in the town. In fact, near the Willowvale

Bleachery stood a large building that was formerly "Fred's Market," and originally was a community hall or clubhouse for the workers. The high school in Chadwicks was built in 1914 and by that time Helene was on her way to stardom.

Helene began acting as a Western star, for she had talent as an equestrian. Her attractive body also won her jobs as an artist's model. Her acting career began with filming for Pathe Pictures in Manhattan and by 1913 Samuel Goldwyn had signed her to a contract. She was only 16 years of age. Fortunately, her mother accompanied her to Hollywood.

Helene Chadwick's career began in 1913.

While she started making silent movies in 1916, the peak of her stardom was during the years 1920 through 1925. Her salary was $2,000 a week. When sound was introduced to films, Helene became more of a character actress and during her final five years in show business, "she was reduced to taking roles as an extra." She made over sixty movies with Warner Brothers, Columbia Pictures, 20th Century Fox, Metro-Goldwyn-Mayer and Paramount Pictures.

Noteworthy performances included, "The Long Arm of the Manister," 1919; "Heartsease," 1919; "The Sin Flood," 1922; "Dangerous Curves Ahead," 1921; "From the Ground Up," 1921; "The Glorious Fool," 1922; "Yellow Men and Gold," 1922; "Dust Flower," 1922; "Godless Men," 1920; and "Quicksands," 1923. Her final performance was in 1937 in the movie, "A Star is Born."

One of her memorable movies opened for two days at the Avon Theater in Utica in April 1920. It was Rupert Hughes' "The Cup of Fury." She was the beautiful starlet of artistic and dramatic ability. With short bobbed hair typical of the 1920s, originally blonde, she conveyed an innocent ingénue, yet she had sincere qualities.

A rare Helene Chadwick tobacco card, circa 1925, was found at an auction. Her name was placed in Jonteel magazine advertisements for face powder, lipstick crème, and in 1920, for the "Jonteel Chadwick Garden Perfume Cosmetic" in Ladies Home Journal. Her picture was on the cover of *Picture Play Magazine, Silverscreen* and *Movie Weekly* in 1922.

In 1921, Helene married William A. Wellman, an American pilot cited for bravery in World War I and who began directing movies. His main accomplishment was the Academy Award winning movie, "Wings." The marriage lasted only two years, ending in divorce on charges of desertion and non-support. They had no children.

Helene's death was attributed to stumbling over a chair and injuring her left side and eye. "She had a highly nervous state." She died in St. Vincent's Hospital in Los Angeles on September 4, 1940 at the age of 42. Helene is buried in Sauquoit Valley Cemetery where there is a large Chadwick memorial.

Janice Trimbey Reilly

CATHERINE FRANCES MILET BUCKLEY

was born March 5, 1898, on her grandfather's farm near Madison, N.Y., the daughter of Patrick F. Milet (1870-1921) and Frances Agnes McNeil Milet. Catherine was the oldest of five children: Neil, Helyn, Agnes and John. Her family moved to Utica in 1900, where her father became a salesman for the Gulf Brewing Company. Patrick, born in Brooklyn had moved upstate and married Frances McNeil of Oriskany Falls, N.Y.

Catherine began her education at St. Mary's School on South Street, then attended Roosevelt School, finally graduating with the first class at St. Francis de Sales Grammar School. Then she attended Utica Free Academy and Geneseo State Normal College in 1917. She was just 19 years old.

For the next four years, Catherine taught in the Utica Schools before teaching at Geneseo while taking graduate courses at the University of Rochester. Catherine returned to Utica when her father died in 1921. She taught kindergarten at St. Mary's School, then second grade at Brandegee School, kindergarten at Egbert Bagg School and Kemble School and fourth grade at Roosevelt School. She also taught Americanization classes for the Bossert Corporation, taught at the Utica Night School and was Director of Chancellor Square and Roosevelt Playgrounds. In all these positions, she worked with many immigrant families who came to Utica to build a better life.

Catherine married City Judge John T. Buckley (1886-1936) on June 29, 1927 at St. Francis de Sales Church. John's father, also named John Buckley was born in Ireland and came to the U.S. as a boy and became a very successful horseshoer. He married a Margaret Buckley, not related to him and they had four children. Judge Buckley, their oldest child, attended Assumption Academy graduating in 1902. In 1905, he entered the law office of Judge M.H. Sexton before entering Georgetown Law School in Washington, D.C. He graduated in 1908 and passed the New York State Bar the same year. He ran for City Judge in 1911 at age 29.

Catherine was active in the Catholic Women's Club, which had purchased the mansion at 294 Genesee St. in 1918 for its headquarters. The first part of the house was built in 1826, with a major addition in 1866. The interior, as well as the elegant gardens surrounding the building, had been well maintained. Catherine would serve as president and was always an active member. Catherine became involved with the Girl Scout movement, which began nationally in 1912, and came to Utica soon after.

Catherine Buckley photo from Builders of Utica in 1941.

With her husband's tragic death July 30, 1936 at age 50, Catherine, became a single mother with two young children. There was a three year old daughter Margaret and a six month old son John to nurture. She was appointed Deputy Oneida County Clerk on January 1, 1939, a position she would hold for the next 32 years. Her responsibilities included the challenge of reorganizing, cataloging and preserving immigration records that began in 1805. During her 11 successful terms, Catherine created a nationally recognized Naturalization Office.

During these years that she was raising up her two children, she held a full-time position and continued participating in community organizations. When the book *Builders of Utica* was published in 1941, the forward stated that the 115 individuals named were "were men and women who stood out among the 102,000 Uticans." Of the 115 individuals honored, Catherine was one of the three women profiled. The citation below her picture says:

> *"Catherine M Buckley, Deputy County Clerk in charge of Naturalization, Past President of Catholic Women's Club, Women of Rotary, the Ladies of Charity of St John's Orphans Asylum, Christ Child Society, the Guild of St Elizabeth's Hospital, Foreign Policy Association, Young Women's Republican Club, Incorporator of the Women's Republican Club of Utica and Oneida County. Member of American Legion Auxiliary, Post 227, Girl Scout Council, Americanization Council. Married to the late Judge John T. Buckley, June 29, 1927, Children, Margaret Agnes and John Timothy, 3rd ..."*

Her interest in those wishing to be naturalized as U.S. citizens went far beyond her job. She helped tutor those who needed help to qualify for citizenship, helped get forms filled out and went into the community to encourage new citizens. At the time of her retirement in 1969, Catherine had processed about 7,000 naturalization petitions, in addition to passport, visa, foreign student and related naturalization proceedings that were conducted by her office.

After retirement, Catherine, now 71, continued her involvement in the community. She became the President of Women of Rotary and convinced the group to buy flags for each new citizen at their Naturalization Ceremony. Catherine had established the practice of having a celebration following the ceremony held during a Supreme Court session at the Oneida County Courthouse.

Catherine entered the Charles T. Sitrin home following surgery for a leg ulcer in her mid 90s. She died January 11, 1996, age 97. Her funeral was from the Church of Our Lady of Lourdes in Utica, on January 15th. She is buried next to her husband in St. Mary's Cemetery, Clinton.

Catherine's impressive legacy includes her two children. Margaret Buckley is a teacher and Principal of General Herkimer Magnet School, a member of the Utica Board of Education, BOCES Board member, and member and President of the Junior League of Utica, Her son John, became a lawyer and at the time of his death in 2013 was Associate Justice of the New York State Supreme Court, Appellate Division.

Jane Sullivan Spellman

MARY CORNELIUS WINDER

was born April 17, 1898, on the Onondaga Reservation, south of Syracuse, N.Y. the daughter of Wilson Cornelius (1870?) and Julia Carpenter Cornelius (1873-1930). Mary's only sister Delia was born in 1900 and would live until 2003, age 103. Both were part of the Wolf Clan.

Mary had little formal education and spoke only the Oneida language until she went to school, but she was always looking for ways to educate herself. She was close to her blind grandmother who shared her knowledge of herbs with all their healing properties and inspired her with stories of the Oneida people. As part of her culture, women had a high status since lineage came down through the mother and clan mothers selected the chiefs.

Mary married Samuel Winder (1893-1972) in 1914. Sam was born in Wilkes-Barre, Pa. and had moved to Syracuse in 1912. He was a self-employed carpenter. They had eight daughters and two sons: Marion (born c1915), Virginia (1917), Florence (1918), Mamie (1921), Gloria (1928), Samuel Jr. (1931), William (1933), identical twins Mary and Elizabeth (1935) and Ramona (1937). Their oldest child, Marion, died at age five but the nine others married and gave them forty-eight grandchildren.

Mary Winder with oldest daughter Marion during European tour c. 1917.

Mary became part of a group that toured Europe just before World War 1 as Europeans were fascinated by the Native American culture. She took Marion with her on this trip. The group wore traditional clothing and performed cultural songs and dances. They were returning from Europe and were to sail on the Lusitania but took the sister ship, the Mauritania. The Lusitania was sunk with all lost on that voyage.

There was never a lack of work for Mary with her large family, including her father who is listed living with the family in the 1930 and 1940 Federal Censuses. She ran a grocery on the Onondaga Reservation in 1920, catering to the 60 Oneida families living there. Mary's hospitality to travelers and people with domestic problems was legendary and her home was often a refuge. (This small hospitable home is now on Oneida lands, next to the Shako:wi Cultural Center.) She baked her own bread and made the children's clothes. Her gardens both vegetable and flower, were extensive. She served as a mid-wife. She was always ready to help neighbors in need.

Mary's skill as a basket weaver and her ability to teach others, kept this craft flourishing. She was a charter member of the Six Nation Agricultural Society that ran the Indian Village at the New York State Fair beginning in 1928.

Mary took up the mission from her father of winning recognition of the Oneida Nation's right to thousands of acres of ancestral land guaranteed to the Oneida People in the 1794 Treaty of Canandaigua.

In 1920, she wrote her first letter to the Indian Bureau asking Washington how much money was owed the Oneida Nation for the use of their land. She received no response but she persisted over the next 30 years to keep the issue alive. There were trips to Washington, Chicago, Albany, Syracuse and Utica, which she managed without owning a car. In 1943, she petitioned the Indian Superintendent in New York State to reinstate Indian land. She was part of a group formed to put in land claims with the Indian Claims Commission, when it was established in September 1946. In 1948, Mary wrote the Bureau of Indian Affairs requesting payment or return of the lands taken from the Oneida Nation by illegal sales done by New York State between1785 and1840. Her letters reminded our national government of the role the Oneida's played in the American Revolution. They were the only Native American group to fight on the side of the Patriots. Mary saw the need to organize all the Indian Nations providing a unified front in presenting claims. Her hope to include the

Oneida people and others from Wisconsin, Canada and northern New York required her to journey to these places and use her skill in uniting all in getting lands returned.

Mary developed lung cancer and moved to Bath, N.Y., where she died at age 56 on June 11, 1954. She is buried in Onondaga. Although Mary did not see her work achieve total success, her children, grandchildren and great-grandchildren and as well as future generations, benefit from her courage and leadership.

Her children continued her ambition. Daughter Florence married Robert Chrisjohn (1921-1991) a wood carver, stone carver, silversmith, an artist so dedicated to keeping the Oneida culture thriving that the Cultural Center, dedicated in February 1993, was given his Indian name SHAKO:WI which means "He gives." This beautiful hand-crafted building was designed and built by Beaver Creek Log Homes, owned by Oneida member Jules Obomsawin. Using massive pine logs, the building has no nails or glue holding the logs together, and the handsome interior has many exhibits showing the Oneida people's creativity and history.

Her daughter, Gloria, married Arthur Halbritter and she continued her mother's vision. Gloria's son, Ray Halbritter, returned to central New York to establish the Oneida Indian Nation, Inc. whose Turning Stone Casino and world famous golf courses have changed the state's economy. Her son Barry and daughter Karen also contributed to the Nation's success in various ways.

Her daughter Mary (Maisie) married Chief Clifford Shenandoah of the Onondaga Nation. She was an artist, tribal historian and businesswoman who continued to follow the vision of her mother to create a homeland for all the Oneida people.

In October 2014, the United States Department of the Interior signed the deeds to 13,004 of the Oneida Indian Nation's current acreage into federal trust. This was largely due to Mary Winder's tireless work.

Jane Sullivan Spellman

GRACE PAULL

was born October 7, 1898, on the farm of her grandfather, Griffith W. Jones, on Grant Road in the Town of Russia, Herkimer County N.Y. Grace was the middle child of Arvin and Hannah Jones Paull. Her older brother Theodore, married Jennie Hardell; her younger sister Sara, married Edward Trevvett. There would be six nieces and nephews (Arvin, Herbert, James and Winifred Trevvett, as well as Gordon and Elsie Paull) that Grace would become quite close to because she herself never married.

Grace's father, Arvin Paull was vice president and founder (in 1917) of the General Screen Corporation of Utica. He was the inventor of a rotary paper screen used in the manufacture of paper. It was produced at the Steam Engine Works in Utica and marketed by Mr. Paull's own company. The screens were used in mills at Beaver Falls and Brownsville. His early adult years were spent in the paper mills on the Black River often traveling as a salesman. Arvin Paull died in his home in Utica of a stroke in 1924.

Grace once said, I took "all art courses made available at Utica Free Academy." Her teacher, Miss Mabel E. Northrup, encouraged her and a number of talented people to draw. Grace attended Pratt Institute of Art in Brooklyn for three years. After graduation she pursued additional studies at the Art Students' League and Grand Central Art School in New York City.

While continuing her studies, she worked on an assembly line, painting cards for Norcross Cards. Grace did commissioned work for them for 25 years, and was 'laid off' when the depression hit. In an interview when she was 89 years old, Grace described her work at Norcross: "Each girl who painted used only one color. We sat at long tables and worked from 9 to 5:30. Samples were displayed to salesmen who selected ones they thought would sell. About twenty artists worked at Norcross at the time."

Grace rose to the position of head designer, painting all-occasion greeting cards, Valentines, Christmas cards, seals, tags and wrapping paper. One of the name tags Grace designed was of Santa playing a grand piano that could be folded to look like a real piano.

It so happened that the Norcross office was in the same building as Doubleday Publishing Company and after showing samples to the editor, Grace was given a children's book written by Margery Bianco to illustrate; the book was published in 1932. Doubleday convinced her to start writing on her own; Grace's dream was to illustrate children's picture books. Later, some of her books were sold at Woolworth stores. "The monetary situation was better and I received full royalty," said Grace in an interview for the *Utica Observer-Dispatch* in 1976.

Authors Grace illustrated for were Clyde Bulla, Ruth Holberg, Mabel Hunt, Carolyn Sherwin Bailey, Elizabeth Coatsworth and Mary Urmston. These books were published by Doubleday, Viking Press and Macmillan Company, among others.

Depicting her childhood experiences, Miss Paull's pen and ink drawings showed characters making maple sugar *(Pancakes for Breakfast),* sliding downhill, picnicking in the woods, sleigh riding, horseback riding, and farm scenes of Cold Brook. "If the

Grace Paull from newspaer photo taken in 1975.

book was a picture book, I would do the works in color. If just straight illustrations, I would use black and white." *Peanut Butter's Slide* (with her nephews as models), *A Horse To Ride* and *A Squash for the Fair* are some of her best examples of at-home works. In those days, Grace came to Cold Brook to work during the summer.

Her books were meant for children – simply written, dealing with all the things that children loved to do, talk about and read about. Of the seventy-six books connected with Grace Paull, fifteen were written and illustrated by her. Some of these were titled: *Four Friends, and They Had a Blue Cart* in 1935; *Gloomy the Camel* in 1938; *Peanut Butter Slide* in 1939; *Raspberry Patch* in 1941; *A Squash for the Fair* in 1943; *A Horse To Ride* in 1949; *A Little Twin and Snowed-In Hill* in 1953; *Freddy the Curious Cat* in 1958; and her final work in 1959 – *Come to the City*. They were obtained in 1973 by the Mid-York Library System. After her death, the collection was given to the Poland Public Library where her very close friend, Frances Warren, was the librarian.

During the time she lived on Washington Square in New York City, Grace completed a lithograph of the square, which was later purchased by the Congressional Library. In Grace's building was the workshop of George Miller, printer of children books and an outstanding lithographer – a handy situation. "She was most famous for her lithography, a process in which the image was drawn on a flat stone with a greasy material that the printing ink would adhere. After printing from the stone, it could be cleaned and reused." These big metal plates were destroyed during WWII – the materials needed for weapons. This lithography process was noted by Gertrude F. Johns in a book she wrote in 1994 called *"Grace Paull, Author and Illustrator of Children's Books."* Johns had firsthand knowledge of Paull's life.

Grace worked mainly in New York City but returned during the summers to Cold Brook. In 1941, Charles Greenidge, a Utica architect, designed Grace's studio, and a neighbor, Lyle Carpenter, built it on the homestead farm where the view from her terrace was breathtaking. A stone fireplace and large windows letting in plenty of light gave Grace inspiration. There was room for her horse, Palamino, to have fields to graze in and plenty of room to plant flowers, which she loved to do. Her brother and sister lived on the farm and raised their families in this country setting.

Grace loved going on picnics with her family – especially to the West Canada Creek, which wound its way through the villages of Herkimer County. There were waterfalls and in the early 1920s and '30s, several covered bridges that made ideal settings. Grace "carried her easel, charcoal, pencils and art supplies with her and after eating a hearty picnic lunch, would sit down and paint. Often she could be seen along the roadside sketching her pictures."

She continued doing watercolor now and then. In 1979, Grace was one of eight artists in an exhibit titled "Realists of Central New York" at Munson-Williams-Proctor Institute. The Munson-Williams -Proctor Institute bought her *October's Bright Blue Weather* for its permanent collection. Miss Paull also made a number of sketches of historic places around Utica including Grace Church, Oneida Square, Plymouth Congregational Church, St. John's Church, General Herkimer's Homestead, Fort Herkimer Church and Baron von Steuben's House, which appeared on post cards. In 1933, Grace drew a lithograph of the Russian Union Church. She was especially interested in 18th and 19th century architecture and a few times local residents commissioned her to paint their homes.

Cold Brook, with a population of 329 according to the 2010 Census, was named after a stream of water passing through. A feed mill sits on the water's edge; it was built in 1857 and put on the New York State Register of Historic Places in 1974. The two-story wood frame structure on Main Street still stands. Originally, the stone grinder and sheller were water powered. The stream once provided water power for a chair factory, button-mold factory, a saw mill, hoe-handle mill, cheese-box factory, distilleries and a door and sash mill. The distillery in 1818 was also used for distilling peppermint, wintergreen, hemlock and other essences.

Grace acquired the mill in 1954. When she finally moved back to Cold Brook in 1965, after spending forty winters in the big city, she converted the building into an art gallery and antique shop, leaving as much of the original mill equipment in place. "I just sold my own work there – books and greeting cards but soon a friend advised me to buy a variety of gift items" like stationery, dishes and postcards. Grace also took other artist's work on consignment.

Several years before she died, Miss Paull sold the Old Feed Mill Art Gallery and her yellow house next to it, but she kept the privilege of living in the house. Her house is now privately owned. Miss Grace Paull died of coronary disease in St. Elizabeth's Hospital at the age of 91 on August 17, 1990. Her interment took place at the Prospect Cemetery. She outlived both her brother and sister.

Legatees in her will, which was probated the following month, mentioned a special friend, Betty Allan. Also in her will were Thomas Deborah, Paul, James, Christine and Amy Trevvett, Sandra and Irving Hall, Anne Hall Pothamus, and Mary and Clyde Palmer. Grace generously left the Russia Union Church and the Cold Brook Methodist Church each a sum of $1,000. Smaller bequeaths went to the Poland Fire Department and the Poland Library.

The Poland Library holds many of Grace's books, now out of print, and six original paintings. The Piseco Lake watercolor was donated through the auspices of the Coonradt family. The central school's teachers association presented the watercolor of Miss Paull's red studio.

Grace Paull was an integral part of the Cold Brook community. She leaves a legacy to be remembered.

Janice Trimbey Reilly

ELLA LOUISE WATERBURY

was born in Oriskany on November 21, 1899, the daughter of Mark Henry Waterbury and Charlotte Rausch Waterbury. She was the great-granddaughter of Henry Waterbury, the founder of H. Waterbury and Sons, Papermaker Felts. Ella had two younger siblings; a sister, Carol Waterbury Campbell and a brother, Mark H. Waterbury, Jr.

She attended the Oriskany Graded Union School and then graduated with highest honors from Utica Free Academy in 1917. She continued her education at Smith College in Northampton, Massachusetts and graduated in the class of 1921. Subsequently, Ella went on to receive a Master's Degree in English from Columbia.

In 1936, meetings were held to encourage and support the establishment of a public library in the village of Oriskany. One of the leading proponents of this venture was Ella Waterbury. On August 6th, the 159th anniversary of the Battle of Oriskany, the Village Board of Trustees voted that a public library be established for "free use of all inhabitants of the village," and they appropriated $50.00 for a ten month rental of an abandoned gas station that had to be moved in the spring. By November, the Library Board

Ella Waterbury in her Smith College graduation picture 1921

of Trustees was established and officers elected. Miss Ella Waterbury was elected secretary, a position she held for 31 years. By December, the Holland Patent Library and several private libraries had donated books. A small laundry stove, one-half ton of coal, and a coal box were donated, as well as were the services to erect the shelves, paint the inside with a quart of cream-colored paint and to ready the building for opening. The National Youth Administration supplied a youth librarian for 20 hours every two weeks at no cost to the board of trustees. A company working on village streets agreed to move the acquired building and a house-to-house canvas was conducted to raise funds. On December 15th, 1936, the books were moved in and the youth librarian, Philip Coolie, sorted, classified and arranged them on shelves. The library was opened January 12, 1937, with a budget for 1937-1938 of $197.00. During the first month of operation, 556 books had been lent out and all appeared to be on the road to success. A large percentage of these accomplishments were under the direction and leadership of Ella Waterbury.

Ella's resolve and dedication to the establishment of the Oriskany Public Library served in large part for the success of acquiring a provisional charter on April 16th, 1937, from the Board of Regents of the State of New York. Soon after this library opened, it set a national record and was declared the smallest library in the United States. Its competitor was another small library in Colmar, New Mexico. The Oriskany Library consisted of 1152 square feet and the New Mexico library consisted of 2400 square feet.

During her tenure on the board of trustees, she offered continual support for the improvement of the library. In 1941, the library was moved to a larger facility and in 1961, joined the tri-county Mid York Library System to better serve the users of the library. When Ella resigned from the library board in 1967, it was accepted with many thanks and much regret. In 1988, a beautiful new and modern library was built not far from the original one, with the good wishes and congratulations of Miss Waterbury.

Her name also appears in other civic endeavors. She was active in bond drives, Red Cross work and as a civil aircraft observer during World War II.

In 1958, the Village of Oriskany had annexed two parcels of land for expansion and development. Miss Waterbury was appointed to the planning board where she served as secretary for over a decade. Her vision, determination and attention to detail were important factors for the success and completion of the projects.

Most of Ella Waterbury's adult life was centered on her obligations to her family and the success and stability of the mill founded by her great-grandfather. She served in many capacities as an officer, treasurer, and a director for almost half a century. The Waterbury Felt Co. was well over 100 years in business and much of the success in the later years could be attributed to Ella's devoted loyalty and her concern for its employees. In 1982, The H. Waterbury and Sons Co. merged with a company in Georgia and Ella retired.

Her death occurred May 23, 1989. She is buried in Forest Hill Cemetery in Utica.

Shirley Tucker Burtch

SILVIA SAUNDERS

was born December 30, 1901 in Clinton, N.Y., to Arthur (1869-1953) and Louise (Brownell) (1870-1961) Saunders, the first of their four children. In spite of the family's seeming isolation in rural upstate New York, the children came in frequent contact with artists and writers of the time through their parents' work and they led eventful lives. Silvia's sister, Olivia (1904-1982), was briefly the first wife of Pulitzer Prize-winning author, James Agee. The elder of her two brothers, William Duncan Saunders (1906-1922) was memorialized after his premature death in a book entitled *Fifteen Years Old*. Her second brother, Percy Blake Saunders (1911-1993), had a very successful law career before his death in Buffalo during a violent confrontation with a burglar.

Silvia's father, Arthur Percy Saunders was born in Canada to English parents. His father was Director of the Central Experimental Farm at Ottawa, Canada, and both his parents were enthusiastic botanists. He was graduated from the University of Toronto and took post-graduate work in chemistry in Berlin, Goettingen, and finally at Johns Hopkins where he received his doctorate's degree. After teaching agriculture and chemistry for several years at Cornell University, he was appointed professor of chemistry at Hamilton College in Clinton, N.Y., also serving as a dean of the college.

He was deeply devoted to Hamilton College and attended all its functions, usually accompanied by his family. He set up a telescope near his home so that college boys might gaze at the stars. He was exceptionally popular with his students who affectionately nicknamed him "Stink" as a result of experiments carried on in the chemistry lab. In addition to his collegiate duties, Professor Saunders had many other interests. Ice skating was a favorite sport; birds were a constant delight. Chamber music was throughout his life a beloved occupation; he played an excellent first fiddle. He was an avid gardener in general and of peonies in particular. In 1931 he issued his first mail order peony catalog, which included his own award-winning hybrids. He continued his professorial duties and many extracurricular activities until his retirement at the age of seventy in 1939. Professor Saunders continued living in the same house, breeding and selling peonies, until his death in 1953.

Silvia's mother, Louise Sheffield (Brownell) Saunders, was born in New York City and attended school there. She received an A.B. degree from Bryn Mawr in1893 and a Ph.D. in 1897. She was a European Fellow and spent time at Oxford University and the University of Leipzig. Later she was appointed Warden of Sage College and lectured in English Literature at Cornell University where she met her husband. After her husband's appointment at Hamilton College, she served as principal of the Balliol School in Utica, New York, tutored privately, and published occasional articles. She was a member of the Hamilton College Chapel, the Association of University Women, and the World Federalists. In 1948 she was awarded an Honorary Master of Humane Letters by Hamilton College. She was also one of the Founders of the Clinton Chapter of Save the Children Federation. Louise Saunders died in 1961 at the Harding Nursing Home in Waterville, N.Y.

Silvia was schooled by her mother until age 18. Hers was hardly what we think of as typical homeschooling since her mother was an exceptional scholar in her own right and had all of the resources of Hamilton College at her disposal. Her father's garden also played a large role in Silvia's education. Besides peonies, almost every garden plant was given a try and there was a constant supply of fruits and vegetables for the family table. Plants that did not thrive in the climate of upstate New York were quickly discarded to make way for better ones. "No one," wrote Professor Saunders, "should undertake the work of hybridization unless he feels within himself an unfathomable well of patience and a strong wall of persistence against which he may put his back when discouragement threatens to get the better of him."

In 1921, Professor Saunders introduced a fragrant, early semi-double dwarf peony which he named after his daughter. Silvia Saunders is a good grower and bloomer, it buds pink, opens blush and blooms white. The center is filled with yellow stamens among which the very bright pink stigmas make a conspicuous pattern.

Silvia spent a year attending lycee in Versailles, France, before attending Bryn Mawr and graduating from Radcliffe in 1924 with a major in music.

After her graduation from Radcliffe, Silvia traveled the United States and Europe as a professional photographer. The stock market crash in 1929 brought Silvia back to New York City where she worked as a designer and lived for a short time with Olivia who was employed in an art gallery. In 1930 she returned to Clinton for a time but continued taking photographs. *A Portfolio of Peony Species* was published in 1934 by the *National Horticultural Magazine.* She published a series of photos in *Hound and Horn* magazine and, later, when she began traveling again, her garden and architecture photos appeared in magazines like *House and Garden.* The *U.S. Camera Annual* featured her photographs twice.

Silvia returned to Clinton again in 1951 to help her father continue hybridizing and run the peony nursery business. In 1960 their catalog featured a phenomenal 70 tree peonies and 120 herbaceous varieties. The nursery also sold seeds and hybrid plants obtained from botanical gardens and collectors in Europe and Asia that were not available from any other source in the United States. The company developed five American Peony Society Gold Medal winning plants, voted by APS Board of Directors for general excellence: Ludovica, The Age of Gold, Chinese Dragon, High Noon, and Cytherea. Four plants also won the Award of Landscape Merit plants for superior ornamental value, overall appearance in the landscape and throughout the growing season, and reliable performance across North America; Cytherea, Ellen Cowley, Lovely Rose, and Merry Mayshine.

Silvia was active and popular on the Hamilton campus,
hosting annual Christmas and
May parties. She performed
in college theater productions
and performed with the YMCA
Modern Dance Workshop. In
1962 Silvia contributed a chapter describing her father's work
to the book *The Peonies,* edited
by John C. Wister. An exhibit,
"Photographs by Silvia Saunders," was mounted by The
Edward W. Root Art Center
at Hamilton College in the autumn of 1966. In 1968 she won

*Silvia Saunders in a photo by
Richard Carver Wood c. 1980*

the Distinguished Service Medal sponsored by the Garden Club of America
and presented by the American Peony Society. In 1970, she was the founder
of the *Paeonia Newsletter,* an international quarterly newsletter for peony hy-
bridizers. Silvia started making efforts to find others to take over the peony
business in the early 1960's but continued to manage it herself with the help of
Francis Affeld until 1976. In 1977 she received the Hamilton College Bellring-
er Award for exceptional service to Hamilton, its alumni and the community
over the course of her lifetime. In the same year Silvia sold the nursery's stock
to Dr. David Reath, of Vulcan, Michigan. Her book, *Isaac Williams, Deacon
and Master Carpenter of Clinton, New York,* was published by the Clinton Historical Society in 1985.

Silvia Saunders never married. She spent her last days at the Katherine
Luther Residential Health Care and Rehabilitation Center in Clinton, New
York, where she died on May 17, 1994.

In 2007 The Emerson Gallery at Hamilton College hosted an exhibition of photographs selected from their permanent collection, "Photographs by Silvia Saunders." The exhibition catalog compared Silvia's botanical studies to those of the German photographer Karl Blossfeldt whose plants seemed to mutate into architectural structures. The Metropolitan Museum of Art, the Art Institute of Chicago, and the Philadelphia Museum of Art all have her work in their collections.

Roberta Seaton Walsh

ALICE CYNTHIA DODGE

was born about 1903 in San Francisco to Dora Mary Allen Dodge and Melvin G. Dodge. The family moved to Utica in 1915 where Alice attended local schools and in 1920 graduated from Utica Free Academy as one of five honor students. She graduated from Mount Holyoke College in 1925 with Bachelor of Arts degree. Alice excelled as a scholar and athlete interested especially in competitive volleyball. Following graduation, Alice was invited to join the Utica Public Library staff by library director Laure Claire Foucher. After a few years, Alice took a leave from the library to study at the School of Library Science at Columbia University from which she received a Bachelor of Science degree in 1932. Then, in 1944, she earned her Master of Arts degree from the Graduate Library School at the University of Chicago.

Upon the death of library director Laure Claire Foucher in November 1944, Alice Dodge was appointed acting director and in 1945, she was appointed to lead the library as director. Under the able leadership of Alice Dodge, the library continued to be a principal educational institution for Utica. Uticans had enjoyed the benefits of a community library since 1825 when a library corporation owned by shareholders was

Alice Dodge from an Utica Observer-Dispatch article December 26, 1946.

located on Broad Street with a collection of 1,100 books. It was 1893 that the Board of Regents of the State University of New York chartered the current library organization. The handsome brick structure, designed by the New York architect firm of Carrère & Hastings, was completed in 1904 at 303 Genesee Street on land given by the Proctor family.

In 1946, early in Alice Dodge's tenure, the library was designated as an official location for international documents and pamphlets published by the State Department of the United States. On the second floor were located departments dedicated to music, religion, philosophy and the arts. The gallery, located on the second floor, offered a regular schedule of exhibitions of art created by local artists as well as traveling art displays. In 1947 the library supported Utica College's development around Oneida Square by designating space within the library to be used exclusively by students and faculty of the college.

In 1952, the library became a repository of microfilms of Utica newspapers. Since the introduction of those easily stored microfilm newspaper records, which extend back to the early nineteenth century, the library has attracted thousands of local and out-of-town researchers and scholars. During Alice Dodge's tenure as director, the Uticana collection of the library increased its holdings of regional historical material, and this collection today continues to grow as a special archive for research on the central New York region.

The Board of Regents of New York State appointed Alice Dodge in March 1952 to a five year term as a member of a state commission overseeing the certification of public librarians. Then in October 1952, Miss Dodge was elected president of the New York State Library Association. The Mid-York Library System was initiated in 1956 to serve Oneida, Herkimer and Madison counties. Mid-York purchased a Bookmobile for Utica which was administered by the library staff during Dodge's leadership. When she retired in 1967 as Director of the Utica Public Library, Miss Dodge had served the library for forty-two years.

Along with leading the library, Alice Dodge assumed leadership roles in Utica community organizations, and in 1981 she was honored to be chosen as Club Woman of the Year by the New York State Federation of Women's Clubs. She was included in Who's Who of American Women in 1959 and 1968. The New Century Club was an institution she valued throughout her adult life, and she held the position of president during 1935-1944. A short time before her death, Alice Dodge gathered historical information to support the nomination of the New Century Club to the National Register of Historical Places administered by the United States Department of the Interior.

In 1943 Alice Dodge became the Superintendent of Plymouth Bethesda United Church Sunday School, a position her father had held. In 1955 she was elected as the first woman president of the Oneida County Historical Society. She was a 50 year member of the American Association of University Women Mohawk Valley Branch, and served as president 1946-47. She was active in the Zonta Club and served several non-consecutive terms as president. Alice Dodge was active in the Mount Holyoke Club, Delta Kappa Gamma, the YWCA, New England Women and the DAR.

Following her 1967 retirement from the Utica Library, Alice Dodge continued to serve public libraries in the Watertown area. In 1968 she took the position of Senior Librarian of North Country Library System in Watertown. She was secretary of Jefferson County Historical Society in Watertown, and active in the Historical Association of South Jefferson.

Alice Dodge died January 4, 1984 and is buried in Adams, N.Y.

Virginia Baird Kelly

HAZEL CRILL PATRICK

was born October 23, 1901 the daughter of Bert H. Crill (1872-1965) and Mary Elizabeth Rasbach (1872-1946) . Their other children included Harold (1900-01), Ruth (1903) and Edna (1909). The family lived in East Herkimer.

Hazel attended local schools and was a graduate of Herkimer High School in 1918 continuing on to New York State College for Teachers at Albany, graduating in 1922. Hazel taught at Middletown and Herkimer before marrying Andrew W. "Pat" Patrick (1905-1969) on July 17, 1926. Once married, Hazel no longer taught.

During the 1930s Pat managed a grocery store on Main Street in Herkimer. Hazel worked there too. This was during the depression when times were difficult for many and the store extended credit to families so that the families could survive.

Hazel was always active in the Reformed Church of Herkimer that began with the settlement of Herkimer in 1723. She taught Sunday School, was a member of the Woman's Guild, a member of the Esther Circle, on the Board of the World Missions of the Reformed Church of America and one of the first women to serve as an Elder and Deacon. Hazel was also the vice president of the Church Board.

She was famous for the pickles she made from the cucumbers she grew. They were usually sold out before the church bazaar began.

Hazel's involvement with the General Nicholas Herkimer Chapter of Daughters of the American Revolution (DAR) began in 1948. She served two terms as Regent and held most of the positions in that organization. As a member of the order of the Eastern Star, Hazel served as Deputy Grand Matron for the 15th District and was Royal Matron of the Crown Court Order of Amaranth.

In 1951 Hazel became active in the Herkimer County Historical society and used her interest in genealogy to answer letters sent to the society asking about ancestors. She could trace both parents back to the Palatine settlement in 1723. The carbon copies of her hundreds of responses are an important part of the Society's collection. Hazel served on the Board of Trustees, acting as secretary for many years. She held the title of Librarian.

Hazel's genealogical genius was challenged when the society was given nine cartons of material on the Bellinger Family in 1974. Society member Tom Bellinger convinced Hazel to organize this material and he contacted family members to raise the money for a book by preselling it in advance. Hazel indexed the material and when the *Mohawk Valley Bellingers and Allied Families* by Lyle

Hazel Patrick from a photo taken in 1989.

Frederick Bellinger came out in 1976, Hazel had an index of over 5,000 names. Working with material that had been published in the *St. Johnsville's Enterprise and News* from 1947-51, Hazel edited and indexed material and the Society published the *Mohawk Valley Petrie and Allied Families* in 1979. She worked with Marion Kofmehl to produce the *Mohawk Valley Harters and Allied Families* in 1981. The *Mohawk Valley Kast and Allied Families* was published in 1985. Her own family was described in the *Mohawk Valley Rasbachs and Allied Families* in 1986 and the *Mohawk Valley Herkimers and Allied Families* in 1989. The last book was done when Hazel was 88 years old.

Also, Hazel went through the old newspapers in the society's collection to take out marriage and death notices. Each event went on a file card and she alphabetized these cards which are still used daily by people looking for information about their ancestors at the Herkimer County Historical Society. When George Hildebrant did a cemetery survey and made a card for each stone, Hazel alphabetized these and they became another resource used daily.

Hazel's husband died December 22, 1969. She continued to live in their home on Pine Grove Road where her gardens, both flower and vegetable, flourished. Her cats and dogs were important in her life. She used her skill in making doll clothes every year to raise money for the church's missions.

At age 92, Hazel decided to move to the Mohawk Homestead where she felt she would be more independent than living in her house in the county. There she was busy organizing card games and putting the borders on jig saw puzzles so the "old ladies and men could fill in the middle."

Hazel died September 8, 2000 at Valley Health Services. Her funeral was at the Reformed Church on September 14th and she is buried in Oak Hill Cemetery in Herkimer. Her wishes were to remember the Herkimer Reformed Church, the Herkimer County Historical Society and the Herkimer County Humane Society.

Jane Sullivan Spellman

FRANCES MESSERSMITH MINER

was born April 23, 1905 in Plainfield, N.J., the daughter of Ralph Kinny (1877-1968) and Charlotte Messersmith (1877-1908) Miner. Ralph was the fourth generation to live in upstate New York and was living with his Uncle William in Plainfield, when he met Charlotte and married her. Frances's mother died December 23, 1908 giving birth to a daughter Lois who only lived a month. Frances' father brought her to live with her grandmother Elizabeth Kinny Miner in Oriskany Falls. Her father married Mina King in 1912 and the family grew with the birth of sister Marion in 1914 and brother Charles in 1919.

Francis attended the local schools and graduated as Valedictorian of her high school class in 1923. Her father as president of the Board of Education presented her with her diploma.

Frances Miner from her Smith College Class of 1927.

She entered Smith College in Northampton, Mass. where in her freshman year she was introduced to botany. The Smith College campus is renowned for its gardens and all trees and plants are identified throughout the campus. Frances graduated in 1927 and her first job was working for the Girl Scout Organization in Elmira, N.Y.

In 1930 Frances began working at the Children's Garden at the Brooklyn Botanical Garden as an educational assistant. She joined Ellen Eddy Shaw who had the idea of using land for urban children to grow plants. Frances picked up this wonderful idea and taught many generations how to take the responsibility of planting, caring for and harvesting their gardens.

In 1959, she wrote a 94 page book *The Adventure Book of Growing Plants.* The opening chapter is titled "Plants Have Secrets", and she writes " If you could look at a different kind of a flower every second, without stopping to eat or sleep, you would need almost two days and eight hours of the next day to see them all. Of flowering plants alone, there are about 200,000 kinds. You will do very well to become acquainted with a few dozen.… The best part of getting to know plants is the surprise you will have discovering the marvelous ways they have developed. Each has some special way of staying alive and of passing life on to the next generation."

Her Saturday classes were very popular and her discipline was strict: Tools must be kept clean, all were to be on time and work hard while they were at classes. Somehow the children loved the discipline and the knowledge she shared.

In 1964, Smith College began the tradition of selecting five alumnae each year to present them the Smith Medal of Honor. Frances was one of the first five selected for her work. Her Smith Medal citation read:

"Frances Miner '27, M.A. New York University '42, is Deputy Director of the Brooklyn Botanic Garden, where she has been for 43 years, and since 1945 Curator of the Department of Instruction. She had introduced thousands upon thousands of children and adults to the wonder of plants life, arranging class visits, lectures in Botany and Horticulture and practical greenhouse experience. Each summer she has encouraged several hundred children to cultivate their own plots at the Botanic Garden and raise flowers and vegetables for home use. Brooklyn under her leadership has been the model and pioneer also in adult education, and now offers 30 courses to 1800 adults every year."

In 1973, Frances retired to Oriskany Falls and built a house overlooking the golf course her brother Charles owned. She became a part of the community again. She was active in Smith College Club activities and was a "super sales person" in the annual pecan sale, raising money for scholarships.

In 1992, when Frances lost her sight, she moved to the Lutheran Home in Clinton so she could be independent. Totally blind, she was known for her pretty flowered dresses and a room crowded with plants. She impressed her visitors with her happy disposition.

Frances died January 17, 2000 in Clinton. At her request she was cremated. She wanted no services. Her ashes are buried in Oriskany Falls. A memorial service was held at the Brooklyn Botanic Gardens. Her brother Charles, sister Marion with their spouses and her nephew attended.

Jane Sullivan Spellman

JOSEPHINE YOUNG CASE

was born February 16, 1907 in Lexington, Massachusetts the only daughter of Owen D. (1874-1962) and Josephine Sheldon Edmonds (1870-1935) Young. She had four brothers: Charles Jacob (1889-1987), John (1902-1922), Philip (1910-1922) and Richard (1919-2011).

The Cases could trace their ancestry back to the Palatinate on the Rhine region in Germany. They fled war and religious persecution eventually landing in New York in 1710 settling first along the Hudson River and eventually near the Mohawk River farming for over 200 years.

Josephine who went by "Jo" was close to her family and influenced by them. Though she lived in many places she always considered her home to be her father's native village, Van Hornesville. Her father, Owen D. Young, was a major figure in American enterprise in the first part of the twentieth century. He helped to guide the General Electric Company to become a leader in speeding the mass electrification of farms, factories and transportation systems. At the request of the U.S. government he created the Radio Corporation of America (RCA) in 1919, helping it to become the largest radio company in the world (the up and coming technology of its time).

Owen D. Young was named *Time Magazine's* "1929 Man of the Year" after working on the Young Plan to help reduce Germany's World War I war reparation penalties. He served as counsel for five presidents. In 1946 at the request of New York Governor Thomas E. Dewey, he headed the commission that laid the groundwork for the State University of New York system. He consolidated the small rural schools around his hometown of Van Hornesville that became the first central school in New York State and the school was renamed Owen D. Young School in his honor.

Josephine Sheldon Edmonds Young, Josephine's mother shaped her children's principles as well as tastes by example. She had attended St. Lawrence University for two years and received her degree from Radcliffe College in 1896. In tending to five children and several establishments, she created a successful environment for Owen to be a "man of affairs" to the outside world.

Jo attended the Brearley School of New York City for her junior and senior high school years. She graduated in 1924 and received a "First Scholarship" to Bryn Mawr in Pennsylvania. She was class president during her junior year there and graduated cum laude in June 1928 with a major in Greek. The college was honored to have her well-known father deliver the commencement speech.

Josephine married Everett Needham Case (1901-2000) on June 27, 1931 at the Universalist Church of Van Hornesville, a faith community her family was involved in since its inception. The marriage ceremony took place after the first commencement of the Van Hornesville School.

Everett was a Plainfield, N.J. native and a 1922 graduate of Princeton University. He was taking graduate courses in American History at Harvard in 1927 when he went to work for Owen D. Young as his personal assistant. From 1929 to 1933 he was assistant secretary of General Electric.

Josephine and Everett had one daughter Josephine Edmonds Case (1932-2010) and three sons: James born in 1935, James Herbert III born in 1939 and John Philip born in 1944. Daughter Josephine would develop skills in editorial work spending 25 years at various institutions in New York City including the Metropolitan Museum of Art and the New York Public Library. With her husband, E. Robert Mason she edited *Herkimer County at 200* published by the Herkimer County Historical Society in 1992.

In 1933 the Case family moved to Cambridge, Mass. to continue their post graduate studies. Josephine attended Radcliffe College and received a Master of Arts Degree in American Literature in 1934.

In 1938 Josephine joined the Skidmore College in Saratoga Springs as a member of its Board of Trustees. From 1960 to 1971 she acted as its chair. At her very first meeting, the decision was made to move the campus to a new site. Before the first building was even completed, Skidmore's president died suddenly and Josephine stepped in to serve as Acting President for fifteen months from 1964 to 1965. For

Josephine Case as President of Skidmore College from 1964 to 1965.

her many years of service, Skidmore dedicated its Case College Center to her in 1974.

From 1942 to 1962 while her husband was President of Colgate University in Hamilton, N.Y., Josephine had an integral role in life of the school community. She taught Literature and found time to devote herself to her passion for writing.

From 1962 to 1969 living in New York City, Everett was President of the Alfred Sloan Foundation and Josephine enjoyed teaching English at New York University. In 1961 Josephine herself became the first female director of RCA and remained in the post until 1972.

Josephine and Everett had a long history of traveling. A few months after their wedding in October 1931 they were invited by the Institute of Pacific Relations to be the American delegates to an international conference at Shanghai and spent two months in China. In 1966, President Lyndon Johnson appointed Josephine as the only woman on the National Advisory Committee on Foreign Assistance Programs. He sent Josephine as his personal representative to investigate the effectiveness of humanitarian projects in Third World countries in South America, the Far East, and North Africa.

In addition, Jo served on the Bryn Mawr Board of Trustees, the Fund for the Advancement of Education, and the National Merit Scholarship Corporation. From 1948 to 1953, she was also a member of the National Board of the Girl Scouts of USA and was president of the Madison County Girl Scout Council. She was on the board of the Saratoga Performing Arts Center in Saratoga Springs, N.Y. in the mid 1960's. In 1970 she became the first woman elected to the Colgate University Board of Trustees. Honorary Degrees were given to her from Elmira College, St. Lawrence University, Skidmore College, and Colgate University.

Jo was tall at 5'8". She loved art, especially tole painting. She liked music, but wasn't musical being tone deaf. She enjoyed teaching and as a warm and friendly person was interested in the people around her. Despite her many endeavors and accomplishments, Josephine considered herself a poet and writer first. Her published works include: *At Midnight on the 31st of March* (1938 is a psychological fantasy set in a village like Van Hornesville told in narrative blank verse.*Written in the Sand* (1945) is a historical novel of the invasion of Tripoli (North Africa) by American forces trying to suppress the Barbary pirates and rescue the Americans they held prisoner. *Freedom's Farm* (1946) is a poetry collection whose title poem was dedicated to her father on his 70th birthday. *This Very Tree* (1969) is a novel about the life and growth of a small country college in New York State. *Owen D. Young and American Enterprise: A Biography* (1982) is a biography of her father in which her husband collaborated. After her death, *New and Selected Poems of Josephine Young Case* (1992) is a collection of her poems published by her husband.

Josephine Young Case died at the Harding Nursing Home in Waterville, N.Y. on January 9, 1990. She was 82. She was survived by her husband, her brother Richard Young, a daughter, Josephine Edmonds Case, both of Van Hornesville; three sons, James III, and John, both of Cambridge, Mass., and Samuel of Fairfax, Ca.; eight grandchildren and one great grandson. She is buried in Van Hornesville Cemetery.

Marjorie E. Sabo

IRENE "PAT" MCCONNELL O'SHEA

was born October 3, 1906 in Utica, N.Y., the daughter of Ambrose (1882-1942) and Francis Kirk McConnell. Irene had a sister, Grace and a brother Roy. Irene was born into a sports family. Her father Ambrose was a major league baseball player from 1908 – 1911 playing second base for the Boston Red Sox and Chicago White Sox. Irene at an early age began following teams, different players and reading box scores.

Irene became a gifted athlete in her own right participating in several sports as a youngster. Upon graduating from Camden High School in 1925, she attended Sergeant's School of Physical Education in Cambridge, Mass. After graduating from Cortland State College in 1928, Irene taught Physical Education at Union-Endicott Central School from 1929 to 1943. Here she developed a strong field hockey program.

Irene married Timothy O'Shea (1908-1939) in 1934 and was the mother of Sheila born in 1936. Timothy died in April 1938. In 1942, Irene moved back to Utica to manage, along with her mother, a baseball team, the Utica Braves. This team later became the Utica Blue Sox. Her father Ambrose owned and supervised the team previously, but upon his death the two women stepped in to manage the baseball team for the next two years.

Irene also worked in the Physical Education Department in the Whitesboro Central School System from 1943 to 1945. In 1945 Irene began her 25 year career at the Rome Public School System leaving her mark as a girls' sports pioneer. She introduced several intramural sports including beginning tennis, archery, soccer, swimming, and bowling. In 1947, Irene also worked for Bill Keating in the Rome City Recreation Department as Program Director. She introduced and organized all daytime activities on the playgrounds including beginning tennis, archery, craft activities, tournaments and special events. Irene also taught at the Rome Women's Club in the early 1950s.

In 1959, Irene was promoted to associate director of athletics in the Rome School System. This move ushered in a new era in girls' athletics. Through Irene's efforts Rome girls had a wide variety of sports to participate in and a large after-school program. Her intramural programs included volleyball, basketball, track and gymnastics. Irene was very dedicated and had a great rapport with both girls and boys. Rome soon became a center of invitational activities and Irene O'Shea's finest intramural teams from Rome Free Academy would be pitted against other schools on a periodic basis. She did not stay long enough to coach in the Girl's Diversified Interscholastic program as she retired in 1970. Irene did however lay the foundation for its establishment. The coaches and athletes of today are reaping the rewards of her efforts.

In 1968 Irene received the Staley Junior High Athletic "Citizen of the Year" Award for diligent service to the girls' athletic programs in Rome. Upon her retirement fifteen women were in Rome's Physical Education Department, 12 more than when she arrived 25 years earlier. Irene had helped form the Rome District Girls' Physical Education programs into one of the state's largest and most diversified. During her career she saw the girls' athletic programs expand to involve 11 sports.

Irene O'Shea was inducted into the Rome Sports Hall of Fame in 1984. She was clearly a sports pioneer although she did not like the label stating "I had a job to do and I did it." At five feet two with fiery red hair and a love of sports, she made a mark both on and off the field.

Irene "Pat" O'Shea picture from Rome Daily Sentinel May 1984.

Irene passed away in March 1990 and is buried in St. Peter's Catholic Cemetery, Rome. In 1996 Irene was inducted into the SUNY Wildcat Hall of Fame at SUNY Institute of Technology at Utica/Rome, N.Y.

Her daughter Sheila Vandeveer of Rome, had stated "I didn't appreciate the magnitude of what mom was doing until I was out of school and could truly see the impact she had." Irene McConnell O'Shea was a woman sports pioneer who paved a path for girls' sports in the central New York region.

Susan Stevens Radell

SOURCES

Ackroyd, Harriet A.

Ackroyd, Harriet A. (1953). "History of the Utica Fire Insurance Company 50th Anniversary 1903-1953." Utica First Insurance Company. [unpublished manuscript].

Bannigan, J. Phil. (1941). *Builders of Utica.*

Internet. Fulton History at www.fultonhistory.com.[articles and obituary].

Interview with Gloria Santucci

Janice Reilly, Oneida County Historical Society

Oneida County Surrogate Office

Nancy Bangs, Utica First Insurance Company, Portrait picture of Harriet Ackroyd by Bacharack

Red Cross Annual Reports for 1942-43, 43-44, 44-45

Tomaino, Frank. "Looking Back into History". *Utica Observer-Dispatch.*

Arnold, Amy Barber

1879 B. C. Butler Map of New York Wilderness–Hamilton County and Adirondack Territory.

Barber, Donald S. (2001). "The Connecticut Barbers, Descendants of Tomas Barber of Windsor, CT."

Charles Herr, Inlet Historical Society, contributor

Donaldson, Alfred Lee. (1921). *A History of the Adirondacks, Volume 1.* Harbor Hill Books. 128-133.

Ely, W. W. (1876). "Map of New York Wilderness to Accompany Wallace's Descriptive Guide to the Adirondacks."

Grady, Joseph. (1931). *The Airondacks…The Story of a Wilderness.* North Country Books.

Headley, Joel T. (1849). "The Adirondack or Life in the Woods."

Herr, Charles. (2009, November 27). "The Otis Arnold Family." *Inlet Historical Society.* Private publication on file at the Town of Webb Historical Association. Old Forge.

Internet. Ancestry.com. at www.ancestry.com [census records, family trees]. Findagrave at www.findagrave.com. [burial records]. Fultonhistory.com at www.fultonhistory.com. [obituaries and news articles].

Murray, Amelia. (1856). "Letters from the United States, Cuba and Canada."

Simms, Jephta R. (1850). "Trappers of New York."

Smith, H. Perry. (1873). "Summerings in the Wilderness or Modern Babes in the Woods."

Thorpe, Thomas B. (1859). "A Visit to John Brown's Tract."

Bagg, Sophia Derbyshire

Bagg, Moses. (1892). *Memorial History of Utica, from Its Settlement to the Present Times. Syracuse.*

Bagg, Moses, (1877). *The Pioneers of Utica From the Earliest Settlement to the Year 1825. Utica.*

"Female Missionary Society of Western District Annual Report 1820" from Oneida County Historical Society

Forest Hill Cemetery Association

Internet. Ancestry.com at www.ancestry.com. [census].

Oneida County Historical Society files vertical files, Utica City directories 1819, 1828

Oneida County Surrogate's file

Patrick Kelly, Oneida County Historical Society

Ryan, Mary P. (1981). *Cradle of the Middle Class: The Family in Oneida County, New York 1790-1865.* Cambridge University Press.

"The Case of Utica NY". Tulsa Law Review. Vol. 4 2004 Issue 4. Article 7. Retrieved from http://digitalcommons.law.utulsa.edu/tir/vol40/iss4/7.

Utica Illustrated 1875. H.R. Page and Company. Oneida County Historical Society

Blackstone, Harriet

1880 Federal Census, New Hartford.

A Mystical Vision: The Art of Harriet Blackstone, 1864-1939. The Bennington Museum, Bennington, Vermont , March 16-June 10, 1984. Catalogue of the exhibit.

Artist file at Munson-Williams-Proctor Art Institute.

Blackstone Family file and Bible. copied by Janice Reilly.

D'Unger, Giselle. *Fine Arts Journal.* Volume 26 Issue 2. 97-101.

House Beautiful. (1905, June)."A Woman's Bungelow" Vol 18. Number One.

Lyons, Channy. (2012, April). "Illinois Women Artists". *American Art Review.*

Obituary. *Brooklyn Eagle.* (1939, March 17). Retrieved from www.fultonhistory.com.

Obituary. *Schnectady Gazette.* (1939, March 17). Retrieved from www.fultonhistory.com.

Obituary. (1939, March 17). *Rome Daily Sentinel.* Retrieved from www.fultonhistory.com.

Obiturary of Emeline Case. (1911, January 20). *Rome Daily Sentinel.*

Obituary of Mills C. Blackstone. (1898, October 11). *Rome Citizen.*

Records at the East Hill Cemetery, Mohawk Street , New Hartford.

The American Magazine of Art. (1918, August). Vol IX #10. 396-405.

Utica Observer. (1926, September 19). [Column about Harriet].

Brandegee, Martina Elemendorf

Santucci, Gloria. (Summer 1952). "Utica's Martina E. Brandegee". *North Country Life Magazine.*

Grace Church, Utica, N.Y. Wes Storn, archivist.

Internet. www.ancestry.com [birth and death dates].

Oneida County Historical Society City Directories and files.

Brandegee, Martina Louise Condict

Santucci, Gloria. (Summer 1952). "Utica's Martina E. Brandegee". *North Country Life Magazine.*

Grace Church, Utica, N.Y. Wes Storn archivist.

House of Good Shepherd records.

Internet. www.ancestory.com [birth and death dates].

Internet records of Trinity College, Yale University and Harvard College

Utica Illustrated 1875. H. R. Page and Company. Oneida County Historical Society.

Brant, Molly

Huey, Lois and Pulis, Bonnie. (1997). *Molly Brant A Legacy of Her Own.* Old Fort Niagara Association Inc., Youngstown, New York.

Rome Historical Society.

Buckley, Catherine Milet

Obituary.

Internet at www.fultonhistory.com [newspaper articles of events].

Bannigan, J. Phil. *Builders of Utica 1941.*

Irene Gilles for Catholic Women's Club records.

Carpenter, Grace Selden Van Wagenen

"Arthur Fuller Carpenter, B.A. 1895." (1945, January 1). *Bulletin of Yale University. Series 1, number 1.* 66.

"A Brilliant Wedding." (1902, October 9). *The Rome Daily Sentinel.*

"Hymeneal." (1917, October 18). *Deruyter [NY] Gleaner.*

Obituary. (1966, March 10). *The Rome Daily Sentinel.*

Rome Arts and Community Center.

Rome Arts Hall of Fame. Web. http://www.romecapitol.com/halloffame.html

"Rome Couple at the Altar: Two Leading Families of the City United." (1902, October 9). *Post-Standard.* Syracuse.

Van Wagenen, Gerrit Hubert. (1884). *Genealogy of the Van Wagenen Family From 1650 to 1884.* Brooklyn, N.Y.

Case, Josephine Young

Carilyn E. Philbrook, President of the Town of Warren Historical Society and Researcher.

Case, Josephine Young. (1945). *Written in Sand.* Houghton Mifflin Company.

Case, Josephine Young. (1990). *At Midnight on the 31st of March.* Syracuse University Press.

Case, Josephine Young. (1946). *Freedom's Farm.* The Riverside Press. Cambridge.

Case, Josephine Young and Case, Everett, N. (1982). *Owen D. Young and American Enterprise: A Biography.* D.R. Godine. Boston, Mass.

Case, Josephine Young. (1992). *New & Selected Poems of Josephine Young Case.* Sutton House.

Cook, Jane. (1990, January 10). "Josephine Case, 82, RCA Board Member and Poet and Writer". *The New York Times.* Retrieved from www.nytimes.com/1990/01/obituaries/josephine-case-82-rca-board-member-and-poet-and-writer.html. May 6, 2015.

"Josephine Case Trustee." (1970, October 11). *Observer Dispatch.* Retrieved from: www.fultonhistory.com. February 2015.

Mc Graw, John. (1992, October 31). *"Josephine Young Case's Hidden Poems Published".* *The Evening Telegram.* Herkimer, N.Y.

"Owen D. Young". (2015) Wikipedia. Retrieved from: http://en.wikipedia. org/wiki/Owen_D._Young. February 20, 2015.

"Skidmore College Leaders." Retrieved from http://skikmore.edu/skidmore-history/centennial/leaders/josephine-case.php. April 2015.

Young, Clifford M. (1947). "The Young (Jung) Families of the Mohawk Valley1710-1946".*The Fort Plain Standard.* Fort Plain, NY. Retrieved from http://threerivershms.com/jungowendyoung.htm.

Chadwick, Helene

1900 Federal Census. New York. Oneida County. City of Utica.

Chadwick Family Bible. Oneida County Historical Society.

Chadwick Family File, Personal possession of Janice Reilly.

"Chadwick Home Fire." (1962, February 4). *Utica Observer-Dispatch.*

Edwards, Evelyn. *Images of America: The Sauquoit Valley.*

Evans, Delight. "A Nice Girl From Main Street." *Vanity Fair Magazine.*

"Helene Chadwick." (2015). Wikipedia. Retrieved from http://en.wikipedia. org/wiki/Helene_Chadwick .

Obituary. (1940, September 6). *Utica Daily Press.*

Notes and pictures from Melvin Edwards, Clinton, N.Y.

Wager, Daniel. *Our County and Its People, Part IIK.* 170-172.

Clapsaddle, Ellen Harriet

Crane, Barbara. (2001, November). "Collector's Corner". *Mid York Weekly.*

D. A. R. Clapsaddle Genealogy.

"Ellen Clapsaddle." (2015). Wikipedia. Retrieved from http://en.wikipedia. org/wiki/Ellen Clapsaddle .

List of heroes at Battle of Oriskany, Tryon County Militia.

"Moore Postcard Museum Exhibit." (2012).

Notes of Evelyn Edwards.

Notes from Jim Parker presentation.

Richfield Mercury. (1905, March 9).

Utica Daily Press. (1934, January 9).

Cleveland, Rose

Dunlap, Annette. (2009). Frank: *The Story of Francis Folsom Cleveland, America's Youngest First Lady.* State of New York University Press. Albany.

Jeffers, H. Paul. (2000) *An Honest President: The Life and Presidency of Grover Cleveland.* Perennial/ Harper Collins Publisher.

Holland Patent More Than a Village 1797-1997. Holland Patent Bicentennial.

Holland Patent Library.

Oneida County Historical Society.

Rose Cleveland. (2015). Wikipedia. Retrieved from http:// en.wikipedia.org/ wiki/Rose Cleveland.

Internet. www.fultonhistory.com [newspaper news and social events articles].

Coman, Charlotte Buell

Aurner, Clarence Ray. (1912). *Leading Events in Johnson City, Iowa, History.* Vol. I: 448. Johnson City: Western Historical Press. Google eBook. 27 Jan 2015.

Brown, P. S. "Charlotte Buell Coman: 1833-1924". Web Blog Post. Women I Wish I Had Known, Part II. At Home in the Huddle. Mar. 2013. Web. 27 Jan 2015.

Burdan, Amanda C. *"Americaines in Paris: The Role of Women Artists in the Formation of America's Cultural Identity 1865-1880"*. Diss. Brown U. 2006. Print.

Burdan, Betty J. (2004, September 6; updated 2008, June 28). "Charlotte Buell Coman-Background and Time Line." Author's library.

E. P. Coman in the U. S. Civil War Draft Registrations Records, 1863-1865. National Archives and Records Administration; Consolidated Lists of Civil War Draft Registration Records. Ancestry.com. 5 Feb 2015.

Ellen K. Baker in the 1870 United States Federal Census. Ancestry.com. 5 Feb 2015.

Ellen Kendall Baker Thompson. *American Art Directory*, Vol. 11:398. Bowker, 1914. Google books. 5 Feb 2015.

Fargo & Bill v. Buell. (1892). *Reports of Cases at Law and in Equity Determined by the Supreme Court of the State of Iowa. Volume 21. State of Iowa.* Google eBook. 27 Jan 2015.

Michael Somple, additional source material.

Mrs. Charlotte Buell Coman (1833-1924). Utica Artists Past and Present. Munson-Williams-Proctor Central New York Artist File. Print.

Portrait of Charlotte Coman. Artist Ellen Baker. (Created 1870). Ask/ART. com. 5 Feb 2015.

William Baker, Missionary at Fairfield and Norway, Herkimer County. (1838). *J of the Proceedings of the Bishops, Clergy and Laity of the Protestant Episcopal Church in the United States of America.* Potter. Web. 5 Feb 2015.

Cone, Sophronia Farrington

Dunn, James C. (1834). *African Repository and Colonial Journal, Vol. 10.* American Colonization Society. Washington: 122, 157. Books.Google.com. Web. 19 Feb 2015.

"Farrington and Johnson Ancestry." n.d. Family Files. Newport History Center.

Greene, John Robert. (2000). *Generations of Excellence: An Illustrated History of Cazenovia Seminary and Cazenovia College, 1824 to the Present.* Greene.

Hyde, Ammi Bradford. (1889). *The Story of Methodism Throughout the World: from the Beginning to the Present Time.* Willey and Co. 561-573. Archive.org. Web. 19 Feb 2015.

Maclin, H. T. "Melville Beveridge Cox (1799 to1833) Methodist Episcopal Church Liberia". 2002. *Dictionary of African Christian Biography.* Boston University School of Theology. dacb.org. Web. 21 Feb 2015.

Park, Eunjin. *White Americans in Black Africa.* (2001). Routledge Press. Google.Books.com. Web. 11 Feb 2015.

Reid, Rev. J. M. (1879). *Missions and Missionary Society of the Methodist Episcopal Church.* Cincinnati: Phillips and Hunt. Archive.org. Web. 12 Feb. 2015.

"The Churches Grow (1817-1843)". (2012). *The Book of Discipline of the United Methodist Church.* UMC Publishing. umc.org. Web. 15 Feb. 2015.

"Milestones: 1830-1860: Founding of Liberia, 1847." *U. S. Dept of State Office of the Historian.* History.state.gov. Web. 15 Feb. 2015.

Cruger, Harriet Douglas

Davidson, Angus. (1953). *Miss Douglas of New York – A Biography.* The Viking Press.

"Gelston Castle." (1989). *Legacy: Annals of Herkimer County,* Vol. 4, Issue 2. Herkimer County Historical Society.

"Lament for a Long-Gone Past." (1957, January 26). *The Saturday Evening Post.*

Dodge, Alice

Dickinson, Alberta J. (1946, December 29). "People Worth Knowing." *Utica Observer-Dispatch.*

Library Journal. (1949, March 15).

Obituary. (1984, January 6). *Utica Daily Press.*

Sarah Bellman. *Utica Public Library.*

Utica Daily Press. (1968, January 22). 22.

Utica Observer-Dispatch. (1984, January 5). 11.

Utica Observer-Dispatch. (1981, May 31).

Utica Observer-Dispatch. (1967, December 7). 8.

Utica Public Library, scrapbook of newspaper articles about the library and Alice Dodge's work as librarian, 1944-1967.

Douglas, Loretta O.

Dickinson, Alberta J. (1945, April 23). "People Worth Knowing." *Utica Observer-Dispatch.*

Giblin, Francis T. (1917, June 27). Written Speech For Principal Douglas [in presentor's own handwriting]. Ilion Free Public Library Archival Records [Ilion High School].

Ilion High School, Ilion Free Public Library Archival Records [folder]

Ilion Alumni banquet held. (June 27,1935). *The Ilion Sentinel.* Retrieved from http://fultonhistory.com

Jean Putch, Ilion Free Public Library archivist

Sweeney, Aileen C. History of the Ilion Central School District. Retrieved January 31, 2015 from http://ilionalumni.com.

"Well-Remembered Ilion Principal Dies in Utica". (1945, October 18). *The Ilion Sentinel.* Retrieved from http://fultonhistory.com . January 31, 2015.

Druse, Roxalana Tefft

Case, Richard G. (1967, September). *The Druse Case: a Folklife Study of Murder.* Thesis. Cooperstown, SUNY Oneonta. Print. Herkimer County Historical Society.

Greiner, James M. (2010). *Last Woman Hanged: Roxalana Druse.* Keene, N.H.: The author.

"March Mention." (1889, April 1). *Norway Tiding* . 2.

Tippetts, W. H. (1885). *Herkimer County Murders.* Herkimer, NY: H. P. Witherstine, Steam Book and Job Printers.

"Ten Years Ago Monday." (1897, March 5). *The Ilion Citizen.* retrieved from http://fultonhistory.com May 4, 2015.

Edsall, Ella M.

Middleville Free Library. Minutes and Archives.

Middleville Literary Union. Programs and Records.

Diffenbacher, Jean. (1990). *Middleville, New York the Story of a Village Centennial of Incorporation.*

Diffenbacher, Jane and Getman,Sara. (2013). *Women of the Kuyahoora Valley.* The Kuyahoora Valley Historical Society. Newport, N.Y.

Obituary of Ella Edsall.

Sandi Zaffarano, Librarian at Middleville Free Library.

Fisher, Welthy Honsinger

"Born Welthy". *World Education.*

Kelly, C. A. 1983. "The Educational Philosophy and Work of Welthy Honsinger Fisher in China and India 1906-1980". Doctorial Dissertation. University of Connecticut . Retrieved from: http://digitalcommons.uconn.edu/dissertations/AAI8319199/. May 6, 2015.

"Our Founder: Welthy Honsinger Fisher".2015. Retrieved from http://www.worlded.org/WEIInternet/aboutus/founder.cfm. May 6, 2015.

Rome Daily Sentinel. (1998, November 14).

Rome Daily Sentinel. (1980, December).

Schugurensky, Daniel. (2012). "History of Education – Selected Moments of the 20th Century". Retrieved from http://schugurensky.faculty.asu.edu/moments/index.html . May 6, 2015.

Swenson, Sally. (1988). *Welthy Honsinger Fisher–Signals of a Century.*

Syracuse Herald American. (1979, May 27).

Welthy Honsinger Fisher. *Biographical Dictionary of Chinese Humanity.* Retrieved from: http://www.bdcconline.net/en . May 6, 2015.

"Welthy Honsinger Fisher". 2015. Retrieved from http://www.worlded.org/ WEIInternet/aboutus/founder.cfm. May 6, 2015.

Harney, Laura Brooks

Harney, Laura B. (1932). *The Skycraft Book.* McCray-Smith Co. Philadelphia.

Perri, Nilli. (2003). *A Renaissance Woman of the Twentieth Century.* Private publication.

Town of Webb Historical Association, Old Forge, N.Y., Photo collection and Harney family file including letters from Laura's son Patrick J. Harney, Jr.

Online Sources: Ancestory.com [census records, social security records], findagrave.com [burial records], futonhistory.com [news articles, obituaries], Northern New York Historical Newspapers - http://nyshistoricnews-papers.org Ninety-Nines, Inc. website: http://www.ninety-nines.org/index. cfm/laurafrancesbrooks.htm.

Herkimer, Catherine Petrie

Patrick, Hazel, Spellman, Jane and Watkins, Williams. (1989). *The Mohawk Valley Herkimers and Allied Families.* Herkimer County Historical Society. Herkimer, N.Y.

Records at the Herkimer County Historical Society. Herkimer, N.Y.

Records of the Dutch Reformered Church. 4 Vol.

Holton, Jessie Moon

"Board of Trustees of the Holton-Arms School." (1980). *Holton-Arms 1901-1980.* Library of Congress Catalog Card Number 80-69651.

Holton-Arms School History. Retrieved from http://www.holton-arms.edu/page.cfm?p=8167. February 2015.

Russia Union Church: 110th Anniversary: 1820-1930. Newport History Center.

Riley Kirby/Personal Files Newport History Center.

Tuttle, L.B. *History of the Town of Newport 1806-1906.* LB Tuttle. Newport History Center.

Jones, Jennie C.

1880 Federal Census, Remsen, Oneida County, N.Y.

1900 Federal Census, Utica, N.Y.

1910 Federal Census, Paris, Oneida County

Waterville Times. (1939, September 14). Vol. 82. #43.

Waterville Times. (1954, March 25). Vol. 97 #28.

Waterville Times. (1941, September 4).

Waterville Times. (1939, July 27).

Ithaca Daily News. (1918, December 12).

Utica Daily Press. (1943, June 26). (1949, December 21).

Clinton Courier. (1946, April 4).

Clinton Courier. (1910, March 9).

Jones, Kate E.

Bellingers, Lyle F. (1976). *The Mohawk Valley Bellingers and Allied Families.* Herkimer County Historical Society. Herkimer, N.Y.

Patrick, Hazel; Spellman, Jane; and Watkins, Williams. (1989). *The Mohawk Valley Herkimers and Allied Families.* Herkimer County Historical Society. Herkimer, N.Y.

Herkimer County Historical Society files for marriage, cemetery, obituary reports.

American Women's History A to Z People Organizations Events. (1994).

Internet, Fulton History at www.fultonhistory.com

Ilion United Methodist Church records.

Women's Relief Corp records.

New York State Redbook.

Photo from Marcia Butgereit, National Secretary WRC.

Keller, Delight Evangeline Ransom

1850 -1930 Census.

Case, Josephine E. (1992). *Herkimer At 200.* Herkimer County Historical Society. Herkimer, N.Y.

Greene, Nelson. (1925). *History of the Mohawk Valley, Gateway to the West –1614—1925.* 4 vols. S. J. Clarke Publishing Co. Chicago. 688-689.

Herkimer County Historical Society, surname file.

Internet, Fulton History at www.fultonhistory.com. [newspaper articles], Find a grave at www.findagrave.com. [obituary].

Kernan, Hannah Avery Devereux

Arnold, George. "Irish Pioneers of Utica in the 19th century." Oneida County Historical Society. [manuscript].

Kernan, John D. (1949). "Notes on the Decedents of John Kernan of Ned County Cavin Ireland and Janie Brady his wife." Utica Public Library. [manuscript].

Kernan, Karen C. Kernan, John D. and Forbes, Robert P. (1999). *Francis Kernan: The Life and Times of a 19th Century, Citizen-Politician of Upstate New York*. Oneida County Historical Society.

Lewis, Clifford and Kernan, John D. (1974), *Devereux of the Leap, County Wexford, Ireland and of Utica, New York: Nicholas Devereux, 1791-1855*. Lewis.

Oneida County Surrogate Office.

Kowalsky, Libby Sherman

Kohn, S. Joshua. (1959). *The Jewish Community of Utica, New York, 1847-1948*. American Jewish Historical Society.

Interviews with Mundy Schapiro, Temple Beth El.

Interview with and picture from Adele Weitzman Sossen, great granddaughte.

Internet. www.fultonhistory.com. [newspaper articles].

Lavender, Ellen Elizabeth

1880, 1910, 1920 Federal census.

1925 New York census.

Cardarelli, Malio J. (1999). *Utica's Mother Lavender: I'll See You In Heaven*. Cardarelli.

Dudajek, David. (1999, November 28). Utica *Observer-Dispatch*.

Internet. *Observer-Dispatch* at www.uticaOD.com. Ancestry.com at www.ancestry.com

New York Folklore Quarterly. (1952).

Obituary. *Observer Dispatch.* (1928, September 8). 14.

Obituary. *Utica Daily Press.* (1928, September 10). 6. [obituary and editorial].

Utica City Directories 1883, 1894, 1899,1903, 1904, 1916, 1924.

Marshall, Helen Curtis

1850, 1855, 1860, 1865, 1870, 1880, 1900 and 1910 Census.

Gaherty, Lillian. (1994). *Happy Birthday Mohawk 150th 1844-1994.*

Herkimer County Historical Society, Surname File.

Little Falls Journal & Courier. (1880, August 17). (1915, October 19).

Obituary. (1910, March 5). *Herkimer Evening Telgram.*

Mather, Mary Ann Buell

1870 Federal Census.

Beers, F. W., and Co. (1879). *History of Herkimer County, N.Y., New York, 1980,* Reprint, Ovid, N.Y.W.E. Morrison and Co.

Benton, Nathaniel S. (1856). *History of Herkimer County.* Albany, N.Y.: J. Munsell.

Mather family letters. Fairfield History Collection, Fairfield, N.Y.

Mather monument. Trinity Episcopal Church Cemetery, Fairfield, N.Y.

Miner, Frances Messersmith

Brooklyn Botanic Garden. (2015). http://www.bbg.org/.

Interview with brother, Charles Miner.

Obituary. (2000, January 23). *The New Times.*

Photo from Smith College Archives , Northampton, Mass., 1927 Yearbook.

"Smith Medal Citation". Smith College Archives. Northampton, Mass.

Munger, Ellen Searles

Christ Church, Herkimer, N.Y. records.

Greene, Nelson. (1925). *History of the Mohawk Valley, Gateway to the West –1614—1925.* 4 vols. S. J. Clarke Publishing Co. Chicago.

Herkimer County Historical Society.

Herkimer County Surrogate Office.

Legacy: Annals of Herkimer County. (1993). Herkimer County Historical Society. Vol 8. No 3.

Interview with Barbara Munger Coonradt, granddaughter.

Oak Hill Cemetery records.

Research by Carolyn Zoller of Little Falls.

Myers, Mary Breed Hawley aka Carlotta

1850 Federal census for Tionesta, Venango, Penn.

1860, 1870, 1880 Federal Census for Hornellsville, Steuben, N.Y.

Bassett, Preston R. (1963, April). "Carlotta, the Lady Aeronaut of the Mohawk Valley". *New York History.*

Bentz, Peter. (2014, July 28). "Area Woman Balloonist Was Adventurous". *Leader Herald.* Gloversville, N.Y.

"Carlotta the Lady Aeronaut". (2013, January 11). Retrieved from https://chriscarnett.wordpress.com/ May 6, 2015.

Case, Josephine E. (1992). *Herkimer At 200*. Herkimer County Historical Society. Herkimer, N.Y.

Dieffenbacher, Jane. (2000, September). "Carl and Carlotta Myers – Aeronautical Pioneers". *Legacy: Annals of Herkimer County*. Herkimer County Historical Society.

Hawley, Elias. (1890). *The Hawley Record*. E. H. Hutchinson & Co. Buffalo, N.Y.

Holden, Henry M. and Griffin, Lori. (1993). *Ladybirds II: The Continuing Saga of American Women in Aviation*. Black Hawk Publishing Co. Mount Freedom, N.J.

Internet, Ancestry.com. Retrieved from http://wc.rootsweb.ancestry.com/cgi-bin/igm.cgi?op=GET&db=eliassillhawley&id=I1730.

Mac Donald, Anne L. (1992). *Feminine Ingenuity, Women and Invention in America.*

Maksel, Rebecca. (2012, August 16). "Carlotta the Lady Aeronaut". Airspacemag.com. Retrieved from http://www.airspacemag.com/daily-planet/carlotta-the-lady-aeronaut-25448637/#jhjQq BCAs5q6ESu4.99. February 2015.

Oakes, Claudia M. (1978). "United States Women in Aviation Through World War I". *Smithsonian Studies in Air and Space Number 2*. Smithsonian Institution Press. Washington, D.C.

Ramos, Richard. (1904). *The Twentieth Century Biographical Dictionary of Notable Americans*. Vol.3.

Recks, Robert. *Who's Who in Ballooning.*

Standbridge, Joanne. Seven True Stories about Carlotta Myers. Storydello web blog. Retrieved from https://storydello.wordpress.com/?=Lady+Carlotta. May 2015.

The Journal & Courier. (1880, July 6). Little Falls, N.Y.

O'Shea, Irene "Pat" McConnell

Internet, Camden alumni at www.camdenalumni.com. [1925].

Rome Daily Sentinel. (1984, May). Rome, N.Y.

Utica O*bserver-Dispatch.* (1999, September). Utica, N.Y.

Patrick, Hazel Crill

Herkimer County Historical Society Records

Internet. Obituary from the Fenner Funeral Home at http://www.fennerfu-neralhome.com/memsol.cgi?user_id=1325183. May 8, 2015.

Patrick, Hazel. Editor. (1979). *The Mohawk Valley Petries and Allied Families.* Herkimer County Historical Society. Herkimer, N.Y.

Patrick, Hazel. (1986). *The Mohawk Valley Rasbachs and Allied Families.* Herkimer County Historical Society. Herkimer, N.Y.

Patrick, Hazel; Spellman, Jane and Watkins, Williams. (1989). *The Mohawk Valley Herkimers and Allied Families.* Herkimer County Historical Society. Herkimer, N.Y.

Paull, Grace

Dieffenbacher, Jane and Getman, Sara. (2013). *Women of the Kuyahoora Valley.* The Kuyahoora Valley Historical Society. Newport, N.Y.

Drahaim, Paul. (1955, January). "Cold Brook." *Utica Daily Press.*

Herkimer County Historical Society, Family Ties.

Herkimer County Surrogate Office, Certificate of Death and Will of Grace Paul #58209.

Johns, Gertrude. R. (1994). *Grace Paull: Author and Illustrator of Children's Books.* Pine Tree Press Publications.

Paula Johnson, Librarian at Poland Public Library.

Obituary. (1990, August 18). *Utica Daily Press.*

Obiturary of Arvin Paul. (1924, December 12). *Watertown Daily Times.*

"People Worth Knowing." (1948, August 1). *Utica Observer-Dispatch.*

Squiers, Luci. (1976, September 26). "She's a Living Legend."
Utica Observer-Dispatch.

Robinson, Corinne Roosevelt

Basloe, Irene. (1989). *Legacy: Annals of Herkimer County.* Herkimer County
Historical Soc.

Caroli, Betty Boyd. (1998). *The Roosevelt Women.* Basic Books,
New York.

Internet. www.fultonhistory.com. [newspaper articles].

Town of Warren Historical Society, various files.

Root, Grace Cogswell

Bottino, Betsey M. (1988). *The Root Glen Hamilton Alumnae Review.*
Vol. 53, No.1.

Grace Root. (1934). *Women and Repeal: The Story of the Women's
Organization for National Prohibition Reform.* LLC.

Obituary. (1975, February). *Utica Daily Press.*

Hamilton College Archives, Catherine Collett.

Interviews with John Root, Eleanor Wertimer, Virginia Kelly, Gordon Hayes
Jr., David Smalley.

Saunders, Silvia. (Summer 1975). "With Simplicity and Sophistication".
Hamilton Alumnae Review. Vol. 40. No. 3-4.

Wilson, Edmund. (1971). *Upstate.* Fs & G. [picture].

Russell, Harriet E.

"Comfortable residence in a charming Victorian setting". *The Mohawk Homestead* [pamphlet].

"Harriet E. Russell's Travel Journal". Ilion Free Public Library Archival Records.

Herkimer County Surrogate Office.

History of the Alumni Association. (1904, June 1). Retrieved from http://herkimer.nygenweb.net/ilion/ihsalumni.html

"Ilion Alumni Book". Ilion Free Public Library Archival Records on Ilion High School [class of 1873].

Ilion Free Public Library. Archival Records [folder].

Ilion Free Public Library. (1899). *Utica Morning Herald.* Ilion Free Public Library Archival Records [folder].

"Miss Harriet E. Russell Leaves The Library Board". (1929, October 24). *Ilion Sentinel.* Ilion Free Public Library Archival Records.

Michael Disotelle, Ilion Free Public Library archivist.

Obituary. (1935, December 24). *Ilion Sentinel.* Retrieved from http://fultonhistory.com

"Old Ladies Home". (1896, December 22). *Journal and Courier.* Retrieved from http://fultonhistory.com.

Spellman, Jane. "Ilion Free Public Library at 100 years". *Legacy: Annals of Herkimer County.* Retrieved from http://herkimer.nygenweb.net/Ilion-FreeLib1.html.

"Three women that played a major role". *Legacy: Annals of Herkimer County* Vol 7. No 4. Herkimer County Historical Society.

"Travelers Club meeting". (1917, October 22). *Utica Herald Dispatch.* Retrieved from http://fultonhistory.com.

Saint Marianne Cope

Ellen M. Benton, St. Joseph and St. Patrick Church, Utica, N.Y.

Hanley, Sr. Mary Laurence, O.S.F, and Bushnell, O. A. (1980). *A Song of Pilgrimage & Exile-The Life and Spirit of Mother Marianne of Molokai.* Mutual Publishing, LLC.

Jacks, L.V. (1935). *The Story of Mother Marianne of Molokai.* The MacMillan Co.

Boughton, Jill A. (2007, February). "Count It All Joy for the Sake of Love – The Journey of Mother Marianne Cope." *The Word Among Us.*

Oneida County Historical Society, T. G. Best Library & Research Center. Utica, N.Y.

Saunders, Silvia

Catherine Collett, Hamilton College archivist.

Picture taken by Richard Carver Wood. Hamilton College Archives.

Obituary, (1994, May 19). *Utica Observer-Dispatch.* 5C.

Saunders, Silvia. "The Work of Professor A. P. Saunders." *The Peonies.* Washington: American. Horticultural Society, 1995. pp. 40-61.

"Silvia Saunders". *History of Exhibitions, Emerson Gallery.* Hamilton College. Clinton, N.Y.

"Silvia Saunders". *History of Exhibitions, Emerson Gallery.* Hamilton College. Clinton, N.Y.

The American Peony Society. web site at www.americanpeonysociety.org.

White, Katharine S. (2002). *Onward and Upward in the Garden.* Boston: *Beacon Press.*

Spalding, Eliza Hart

Drury, Clifford Merrill. (1936). *Henry Harmon Spalding.* The Caxton Printers, Ltd. Caldwell, Idaho.

Drury, Clifford Merrill. (1937). *Marcus Whitman, M.D.* The Caxton Press, Ltd. Caldwell, Idaho.

James, Edward T. (1974). *Notable American Women: A Biographical Dictionary. Volume 111.* The Belknap Press of Harvard University Press. Cambridge, Mass.

Klossner, Joan. (1997). *The Holland Patent: More Than a Village: 1797-1997.* Holland Patent, N.Y.

Squire, Ellen Moss aka Nellie Thurston

1900 Federal Census.

Dieffenbacher, Jane and Getman, Sara H. (2013). *Women of the Kuyahoora Valley.* The Kuyahoora Valley Historical Society.

Morris, Hobie. (2002, November). "Central New York's First Aerial Heroine: Balloonist Nellie Thurston Squire." *Life and Times of Utica.* 14-20.

"Onondaga Fair." (1882, October 13). *The Cortland News.*

Recks, Robert. *Who's Who of Ballooning.*

Records. Gravesville N.Y. Cemetery. Herkimer County, NY

"Squire Article." (1882, October 13). *The Cortland News.*

Stevens, Eugenie

ALS IKH KAN, Old Girls Of Mrs. Piatts School, 1870 – 1892. (1893) Utica, NY. Child's & Son Print.

"Curious Questions Asked." (1911, January 24). *The Rome Daily Sentinel.* 2.

"Death of E. L. Stevens." (1900, November 12). *The Rome Daily Sentinel.*

"Eugenie Stevens Dies on Birthday". (1940, August). *The Rome Daily Sentinel.*

Internet. Find a Grave. Clara Catlin Stevens, 1923; Burial, Rome (Oneida), Oneida, N.Y. Rome Cemetery. Citing record ID 19802299. Retrieved from http://www.findagrave.com.

"Library Economy and History". (1901). *Library Journal 26.* 162-3.

"Library Economy and History". (1901). *Library Journal 26.* 712.

More, David Fellows. *Historical Journal of the More Family. Vol. 1.* Roxbury, NY: John More Association.

Nursey, Walter R. (1912). "Sunday Opening." *Report upon Public Libraries, Literary and Scientific Institutions, Etc. of the Province of Ontario for the Year 1911.* Toronto: L.K. Cameron. 562-3.

"The First One Hundred Years." Jervis Public Library. Web. Retrieved from http://www.jervislibrary.org/jpl_history.html. February 2015.

Waterbury, Ella Louise

Minutes of Oriskany Library Board of Trustees.

Minutes of Oriskany Village Board of Trustees.

Internet. www.fultonhistory.com [newspapers articles covering events].

Obituary.

Oriskany Museum materials.

Photo from Smith College Archives, Northampton, Mass., 1921 Yearbook.

Watson, Lucy Carlile

Clarke, T. Wood, M.D.(1952). *Utica for a Century and a Half.* Widman Press. Utica, N.Y.

"Foes of Suffrage Confident in Utica." (1915, October 31). *The New York Times.* 5.

Leonard, John W. *Woman's Who's Who of America: A Biographical Dictionary of Contemporary Women of the United States and Canada 1914-1915.*

Oneida County Historical Society, Utica. Lucy Carlile Watson Collection, Box 2007.

Twomey, Erin. (2011, May). "The Suffrage Movement through the Eyes of Lucy Carlile Watson." Retrieved from www.utica.edu/academic/ssm/history.

"Women's Suffrage Notes." (1912, August 31). *Utica Herald Dispatch.* 6.

Utica Daily Press. (1914, June 13).

Welch, Kate Loftus

Barnes, Thomas. (1997). *The Poet of Forge Hollow.* Willona Press.

Barnes, Thomas and Welch, Kate Loftus. (1996). *Along Willona Creek: The Country Correspondence of Kate Loftus Welch to the Waterville Times (1898-1934).*

Beetle, David H. (1947). "Along the Oriskany." *Utica Observer-Dispatch.*

Dorothy McConnell, retired Town of Marshall Historian

Doris Stephen, Archivist Waterville Historical Society

White, Adelaide Thompson Williams

1940 United States Federal Census. Web source. www.ancestry.com. 2012.

Chapin, Mary. (2009, March 11)." Alice Paul, a Fitting Figure to Remember during Women's History Month." *Utica Observer-Dispatch.* Retrieved from www.uticaod.com

Cutter, William. (1912). *Genealogical and Family History of Western New York: A Record of the Achievements of Her People in the Making of a Commonwealth and the Building of a Nation.* Vol 1. Google eBook. Retrieved from http://books.google.com/.

"Harry Draper White." (2011). *Empire State Society, Sons of the American Revolution Membership Applications,* 1889-1970 Retrieved from http://www.ancestry.com.

Fitch, Charles E. (1916). *Encyclopedia of Biography of New York, a life record of men and women whose sterling character and energy and industry have made them preminent in their own and many other states.* Boston: The American Historical Society.

Interview with the late Jessie (White) Henze, daughter of Dr. H. D. White and his 2nd wife, Marion B. Fear.

"Mrs. Harry D. White". (July 10, 1917). *Dunkirk Evening Observer.* Retrieved from http:www.fultonhistory.com.

Todd, Helen M. (September 1, 1911). "Getting Out the Vote." *American Magazine.* 611-19.

Williams, Helen Munson

D'Ambrosio, Anna Tobin, ed. (1999). "With Style and Propriety," in *Masterpieces of American Furniture from the Munson-Williams-Proctor Institute.* Utica, NY: Munson-Williams-Proctor Institute.

D'Ambrosio, Anna Tobin, (Spring 1998). "Helen Munson Willliams: The Vision of a Victorian Collector," *19th Century.* pp. 10-16. (The magazine of the Victorian Society in America).

Laura Laubenthal , Munson-Williams-Proctor Institute.

Portrait of Helen E. Munson, 1843 by Frederick Spencer, American (1805-1885), oil on canvas, 34 ¼ x 27 ¼ , Proctor Collection, P.C. 104, Munson-Williams-Proctor Arts Institute, Museum of Art, Utica, N.Y.

Winder, Mary Cornelius

1940 Federal census.

George, Susan Herbert. "Mary Winder: A Full Life With Land Claim At Its Center." The Oneida Onyota A Ka. Oneida Nation News Special Edition.

Internet sources. www.oneidanation.com

Kandice L Watson, Director, Education & Cultural Outreach Oneida Nation, Shako:wi Cultural Center.

Lisa Latocha, SHAKO:WI Cultural Center.

"The Way We Were Images from the Shako:wi Photographic".
Shako:Wi Cultural Center.

Zoller, Zaida

Case, Josephine E. (1992). *Herkimer At 200.* Herkimer County Historical Society. Herkimer, N.Y. 179. [Herkimer County Industrial Directory].

"Herkimer County Humane Society." (1992). *Legacy: Annals of Herkimer County* Vol. 7, No. 3. Herkimer County Historical Society.

Internet. www.fultonhistory.com [articles citing Zaida Zoller's name from 1898-1973].

Interviews with Genie Zoller, great-niece of Zaida Zoller, and Karen Zuis, registrar of Astenrogen DAR Chapter.

Obituaries. Zaida Zoller. (January 24, 1980). *Evening Times.* Thomas Zoller. (November 26, 1952). *Utica Daily Press.* Abram Zoller. (May 26, 1962). *Rome Daily Sentinel.* Maude Zoller. (November 6, 1962). *Utica Observer-Dispatch.* John Zoller. (February 18, 1964). *Utica Observer-Dispatch.*

Portrait by Michael Cariglio of Utica taken from a photograph from 1907. Presented to the Herkimer County Humane Society at the 60th Anniversary Party Celebration in 1973. It has hung there since.

Zoller, Carolyn and Howard, Enid. (2002). *The Mohawk Valley Zollers and Allied Families.* The Herkimer County Historical Society. Herkimer, N.Y.

BIBLIOGRAPHY

Bagg, Moses M. (1892). *Memorial History of Utica, from Its Settlement to the Present Times.* Syracuse.

___. (1877). *The Pioneers of Utica. From the Earliest Settlement to the Year 1825.* Utica.

Beers, F. W., and Co. (1879). *History of Herkimer County, N.Y.,* New York, 1980, Reprint, Ovid, N.Y., W. E. Morrison and Co.

Benton, Nathaniel S. (1856). *History of Herkimer County.* Albany, N. Y., J. Munsell.

___. (1856). *History of Herkimer County, Including the Upper Mohawk Valley.* Albany.

Case, Josephine E. (1992). *Herkimer At 200.* Herkimer County Historical Society. Herkimer, N.Y.

Clarke, T. Wood. (1952). *Utica: For a Century and a Half.* Utica.

Cookingham, Henry J. (1912) *History of Oneida County.* 2 vols., Chicago.

Coventry, Alexander. (1978). *Memoirs of an Emigrant: The Journal of Alexander Coventry, M. D.,* 2 vols. Albany.

Crandall, Charles E. (1954. Reprint 1960). *Herkimer County Commemorative Brochure.* Herkimer, N. Y.: Department of Archives and History.

Durant, Samuel. (1878). *History of Oneida County, New York, 1667-1878.* Philadelphia.

Eisenstadt, Peter. (2005). *The Encyclopedia of New York State.* Syracuse Press.

Hardin, George A., and Frank H. Willard. (1893). *History of Herkimer County.* Syracuse, N. Y.: D. Mason and Co.

Jones, Pomroy. (1851). *Annals and Recollections of Oneida County.* Rome.

Kelly, Virginia B.; O'Connell, Merrilyn R.; Olney, Stephen S.; and Reig, Johanna R. (1972). *Wood and Stone: Landmarks of the Upper Mohawk Region.* Utica .

Miller, Blandina Dudley. (1895). *A Sketch of Old Utica.* Utica.

Nassar, Eugene. (1971). *East Utica: Selections from a Prose Poem,* designed, and with original
   woodcuts by Robert Cimbalo. Utica.

Oneida County. (1977). *The History of Oneida County.* Utica.

Ryan, Mary P. (1981) *Cradle of the Middle Class: The Family in Oneida County, New York*
   1790-1865. New York.

Utica Public Library, compiler. (1932) *A Bibliography of the History and Life*
   of Utica: A Centennial Contribution. Utica.

Wager, Daniel E. (1896). *Our County and Its People.* Boston.

ACKNOWLEDGEMENTS

This project has been in the works for over 20 years. So many wonderful people have contributed to it with money, encouragement and actual writing. Many of them are mentioned in the sources pages. This page will cover the last year.

Lynne Mishalanie, who constantly supported the idea and me, deserves the credit for not letting this project die. Kathie Bishop added her vision and skills in creating a timeline to give the project a form. Judy Gorman added her considerable organizational and fundraising skills to make the project a financial reality.

My colleagues, Sue Perkins and Caryl Hopson, at the Herkimer County Historical Society provided their personal support over the many years. They also used their professional talents to carry out the many tasks that had to be done to make the book possible.

My wisdom in recruiting Barbara Dunadee makes me extremely happy. Any task thrown at her was handled with competence from designing a brochure, taking photos or working out logistics. Her skills in helping those of us with limited computer knowledge were very helpful. Her knowledge, her patience and total support has made it all happen. We called on our mutual friend, Deborah Kidder, for additional help and she gladly assisted.

Jane Sullivan Spellman

Jane Ann Sullivan grew up in Fulton, N.Y. She graduated from Smith College in Northampton, Mass. She worked for the Toledo (Ohio) Girl Scout Council, Degnan & Cook Public Relations Firm in Toledo and the United Community Chest and Council of Syracuse and Onondaga County. In 1969, she married James E. Spellman. In 1973, she became part-time director of the Herkimer County Historical Society. In 1995 and 22 years later, she retired from this position overseeing a staff of four full-time employees and having had the society produce over 20 publications.